INSIGHT

C000095448

BILBAO &
NORTHWEST SPAIN

72-50
7d

Discovery
CHANNEL

APA PUBLICATIONS
Part of the Langenscheidt Publishing Group

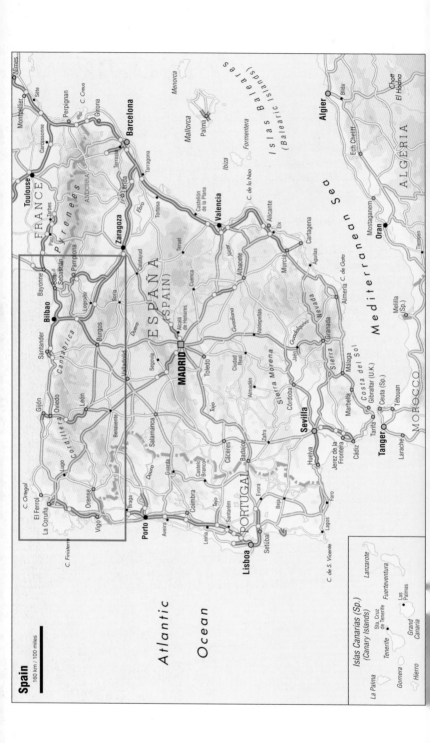

Spain
160 km / 100 miles

Atlantic

Ocean

FRANCE

Pyrenees

ANDORRA

ESPAÑA (SPAIN)

MADRID

PORTUGAL

Lisboa

Mediterranean Sea

ALGERIA

MOROCCO

Islas Baleares (Balearic Islands)

Islas Canarias (Sp.) (Canary Islands)

La Palma   Gomera   Hierro   Tenerife   Sta. Cruz de Tenerife   Grand Canaria   Las Palmas   Fuerteventura   Lanzarote

Welcome

This guidebook combines the interests and enthusiasms of two of the world's best-known information providers: Insight Guides, who have set the standard for visual travel guides since 1970, and Discovery Channel, the world's premier source of non-fiction television programming. Its aim is to help visitors make the most of this immensely rich and varied corner of Spain during a stay of a week or two. To this end, Insight's expert on the region, Nicholas Inman, has prepared a series of itineraries based on the following key areas, working east to west: the Basque Country (itineraries 1–7, Asturias and Cantabria (itineraries 8–10) and Galicia (itineraries 11 and 12). The book begins in Bilbao, the gateway to the region for many visitors, and increasingly popular as a holiday destination in its own right thanks in part to the new Guggenheim Museum. From Bilbao, the book suggests tours of La Rioja and then a drive through the mountains to Burgos with its fine Gothic cathedral and monasteries. It then explores the coast of the Basque country, including fashionable San Sebastián, before moving on to Navarra and then west to the magnificent Picos de Europa and the fine cities of Oviedo and León. The itineraries section ends in Galicia, where Santiago de Compostela draws pilgrims from all over the world.

Supporting the itineraries are sections on history and culture, shopping, eating out and nightlife plus a detailed practical information section that includes a list of hand-picked hotels.

Nicholas Inman has been travelling around Spain since the 1980s, writing about and photographing a country he considers to be a bottomless source of fascination, full of odd stories to tell and unsung places to discover. He is particularly interested in Spanish wildlife and in the off-beat aspects of Spanish life, especially the extraordinarily varied calendar of traditional fiestas. A regular Insight contributor, he now lives in France with his Spanish wife and two children.

Pages 2–3: San Sebastián
Pages 8–9: giants at a festival in Burgos

History &Culture

Y ou could easily drive past the scrub-clad Sierra de Atapuerca, east of Burgos, without suspecting that it concealed anything of particular interest. Yet the caves here have yielded the earliest remains of human beings anywhere in Europe, dating back nearly one million years. Northwest Spain has been continually inhabited ever since, with later generations of prehistoric man settling in close proximity to the coast.

The most famous of all the ancient Spanish sites are the cave paintings at Altamira (in Cantabria), which date back at least 14,000 years. There are less well-known cave paintings elsewhere, at Puente Viesgo (also in Cantabria), Santimamiñe (near Gernika in the Basque Country) and in the Cueva de Tito Bustillo near Ribadesella in Asturias. The purpose of these paintings has never been fully explained; nor has that of the dolmens scattered here and there in the landscape – for instance at La Hoya, near Laguardia (in the Basque part of la Rioja) and at Cangas de Onís (on the edge of the Picos de Europa), where the Ermita de Santa Cruz is built over one such dolmen.

What is known is that, in around 1000BC, the Celts arrived and settled in Galicia, bringing with them their pottery-making skills. At the same time the mineral wealth of the Iberian peninsula began to attract the interest of the trading civilisations of the Mediterranean. But the Phoenicians, Greeks and Carthaginians largely settled the south and east coasts, disregarding the colder, wetter, more mountainous north.

The Romans meet the Basques

Neither did the Romans, the first unifiers of Spain, show much interest in the north, at least not to begin with. It famously took the Romans seven years to bring Gaul under their control, but it took 200 years to conquer Spain. The peninsula was finally subdued in the reign of Augustus, who became ruler of the whole Roman Empire in 31BC. The Cantabrian War (26BC–19BC) led to the subjugation of Cantabria and Asturias, but there are fewer Roman remains in the north than elsewhere in Spain. The most outstanding are in Galicia: the city walls of Lugo and the lighthouse at A Coruña.

The first reference to a race of warrior-like people living on the coast of the Bay of Biscay is in the work of the Roman writer Strabo (64BC–AD24), who gave them the name *vascones*, or Basques. The Basques, who asserted their independence from every passing invader, from north and south, kept no written records before the Romans arrived, and would not do so until 1,000 years after they had gone. Yet then, as now, they staunchly defended their language, culture and freedom.

Left: Celtic stone buildings above Oviedo
Right: early depiction of Basque whalers

There is little doubt that the Basques had existed for several centuries before Strabo's time, to the best of our knowledge in the region they inhabit today, but historians find it impossible to say when the Basques first settled the territory or where they came from. Their language is unrelated to any other and analysis of their blood types and physical features – their generally burly physiques tend to be thick chested and large shouldered, with faces characterised by long, straight noses, thick eyebrows and strong chins – has led to the suggestion that they may be the original inhabitants of Europe, the direct descendants of Cro-Magnon man.

When the Roman Empire went into terminal decline, Spain was overrun by barbarian tribes such as the Vandals, Suevi and Alans. By the 6th century the invading Visigoths had gained supremacy, and it was they who established Christianity as the country's religion. But their occupation was short-lived and early in the 8th century they were displaced by Islamic invaders from Africa – the Moors. As had been the case in previous centuries, the cold mountains of the north did not much appeal to the interlopers; the extent to which they controlled the territory mattered little to them.

In 722, however, a band of Visigothic noblemen and mountain dwellers led by the semi-mythical Don Pelayo ambushed the Moors' army at Covadonga in Asturias. This, the Moors' first defeat on Spanish soil, might have been no more than an insignificant skirmish to the north Africans, but it was a symbolic victory of immense importance to the beleaguered Christians, who saw it as a last-ditch stand on the north coast. After this victory, Don Pelayo created a tiny state for himself, the kingdom of Asturias.

Alfonso the Chaste

Don Pelayo's fledgling kingdom developed quickly under the leadership of Alfonso II (791–842), who was nicknamed El Casto ('the Chaste') as a result of his reputation for morality. Alfonso saw himself as the heir to Christian Visigoth Spain, which had been conquered by the perfidious infidel. It was in the course of his 50-year reign that the tomb of the apostle St James was reputedly discovered at Santiago de Compostela, thereby initiating one of the three great pilgrimages of Christendom (the others being to Rome and Jerusalem). St James, who became known as 'the Moor-Slayer', was wont to put in an inspiring appearance at battles as the Christians fought to win back territory from the Muslims.

A carving looking down on the main square of Santiago de Compostela depicts St James in action. During Alfonso's reign – and to an even greater extent during the reign of his successor, Ramiro I – a series of exquisite churches were built around the Asturian capital of Oviedo. In time Oviedo was displaced by León as the kingdom's capital.

The Christian reconquest of Spain was a slow, laborious affair in which the northerners suffered numerous setbacks, but over the centuries the Christians advanced steadily southwards. Meanwhile a rival Christian kingdom arose in Navarra, whose greatest monarch was Sancho III (1000–35), who was known as

Left: Don Pelayo, scourge of the Moors

history/culture

the Great. Similarly 'great' was the hero of the Reconquest: Rodrigo Díaz de Vivar. Born near Burgos in 1043, he is known to history by his honorific name, El Cid. His adventures were recounted in the contemporary minstrel poem, *El Cantar de Mio Cid*, and, albeit with little in the way of historical veracity, in the Hollywood epic starring Charlton Heston as a muscle-bound El Cid.

United Spain

By the 13th century the Reconquest was all but complete. With the Moors driven out, the focus of military and dynastic events had returned to the south. Having served as the cradle of Christian Spain, both before and after the invasion of the Moors, the northwest became something of a pastoral backwater.

Late medieval Spain saw a series of mergers by marriage and acquisitions by force as counties and kingdoms coalesced into two great power blocs. These two in turn were united by the marriage of Isabel of Castile and Fernando of Aragón in 1469. The stage was set for the conquest of the last Moorish kingdom, Granada, and the unification of Spain. In the same year, 1492, Columbus set sail for the New World, with a number of Basque seamen in his crew. This was the age of discovery, colonisation and the creation of the Spanish Empire. Another Basque, Juan Sebastián Elcano ensured his place in maritime history 30 years later as the first man to bring an expedition around the world, after the death of its leader Ferdinand Magellan.

In reality, the unification of Spain was not completed until 1512 when Fernando's troops annexed most of Navarra – the part that lay south of the Pyrenees. Four years later the Spanish crown passed to a foreigner, Carlos I (the Holy Roman Emperor Charles V) who landed on the Asturian coast declaring, 'I speak Spanish to God, Italian to my wife and German to my horse.' Engaging in a series of wars, he expanded the empire but in so doing he drained the national coffers.

This was the beginning of Spain's Golden Age, which was particularly well expressed in the arts. Cervantes (1547–1616) wrote *Don Quixote de la Mancha*, arguably the most influential novel in the history of Western liter-

Above: St James 'the Moor-Slayer'
Right: the explorer Juan Sebastián Elcano

ature, at the start of the 17th century, and Velázquez (1599–1660) brought a new realism to portraiture, as seen in his remarkable study of Felipe IV. But the term 'the Golden Age' refers primarily to the grandiose ambitions that Charles passed down to his son and heir, Felipe II. While the economy spluttered along, Felipe planned to dispatch a fleet of ships to invade England, the kingdom of his sister-in-law, Elizabeth I. The Spanish Armada finally departed from A Coruña in Galicia in 1588 with its commander loudly complaining about being ill-prepared. What happened next depends on your nationality: the English proudly claim that it was their naval superiority that was responsible for scuppering the Armada in a series of sea battles; the Spanish maintain that their defeat was due solely to the disadvantageous weather around the coasts of Britain.

In the 17th century, Spain's empire and prestige began to decline although the New World, in whose conquest it had played a major role, was still being colonised and developed. To peasants eking out a living in the wet mountains of northern Spain, emigration across the Atlantic must have been an attractive proposition. Those who made their fortunes in South America often returned as rich 'indianos' to build villas for themselves in choice spots such as Comillas, the Basque coast and the valleys of Navarra.

Conservative Carlists

By the 19th century Spain had become a battleground for ideologues and vested interests. In 1813, at the end of the War of Independence (also known as the Peninsula War), parliament drew up a constitution for the return of Fernando VII, but he tore it up and returned to absolutist ways. The resulting struggle, between enlightened liberals and diehard conservatives reflected events that were tearing the whole continent apart. The conservative 'Carlists' rallied around Fernando's brother and established a stronghold in northern Spain. Headquartered at Oñati in the Basque Country and at Estella in Navarra, they fought three futile wars (1833–39, 1847–49 and 1872–76).

The Carlists advocated the restoration of a strong monarchy, the primacy of Catholicism, and the rights of landowners vis-à-vis the peasantry. They were suspicious of cities, industry and modernity, which they held responsible for the discontent and free-thinking that were plaguing Spain. In their red berets, the Carlists are often depicted as romantic guerrillas fighting to bring back an old order in which everyone knew his place. The conflicts smouldered on until they were reignited, and finally resolved, by the Civil War (1936–39).

Isabel II, around whom the liberals rallied, is remembered as the first VIP visitor to San Sebastián (Donostia in Basque) – her visit was largely responsible for putting this new resort on the map. For all the conservatives' resistance, Spain was modernising as fast as it could: in Asturias railways

Above: the ships of the Spanish Armada failed to conquer England

were built and coal was mined. The iron-ore deposits around Bilbao transformed this well-to-do port into one of Spain's principal centres of heavy engineering; the heyday of the city's economy – in the closing years of the 19th century – can be clearly seen in the grandiose buildings that still grace the Gran Vía.

The late 19th century was also a time of rediscovering cultures that had been submerged in the Spanish melting pot. Basque nationalism was defined anew by Sabino Arana, and Galica underwent a *Rexurdimento*, or Revival, that was personified by the poet Rosalía de Castro.

On 12 April 1931 a general election resulted in an overwhelming public endorsement for a republic that was fated to survive only five years before the country was split down the middle. Popular leftist expectations for reform could not be met and in October 1934 a general strike developed into an armed rebellion. The uprising's main protagonists were Asturian miners, who established a revolutionary commune in an attempt to forestall the advent of fascism in Spain. They had guns but little ammunition; their main weapon was dynamite, with which they kept government troops at bay for two weeks. More than 2,000 workers were killed by troops led by the unscrupulous Francisco Franco from neighbouring Galicia. It was a foretaste of what all of Spain was about to experience two years later in the Spanish Civil War.

Franco

Franco was one of the ringleaders behind the military uprising of 18 July 1936, which sought to overthrow the elected government and impose a new order. The uprising divided the north as it did the whole country. Most of the Basque Country supported the government, but Galicia and Navarra immediately fell to the rebels. Franco was a determined, ruthless leader who, despite his reputation as a fascist, was unhindered by ideological baggage. However, his campaign, which was intended to last no more than a few weeks, became bogged down at several points of unexpectedly fierce resistance. Even with the modern firepower provided by Nazi Germany and Mussolini's Italy (who both saw the Civil War as a testing ground for their new armaments) he made only slow progress against the Basques. The capture of Bilbao, with its desirable heavy industry, was a vital strategic aspiration.

Perhaps it was the need for an easy victory that prompted the most controversial incident of

Above: an early photograph of San Sebastián
Right: Basque industry extolled 100 years ago

the war: the saturation bombing of the unprotected market town of Gernika in April 1937. This atrocity later inspired Picasso to create *Guernica*, his masterpiece of anti-war propaganda. Four months later the Basque Country fell to the rebels but the Civil War ended only in 1939, on the eve of World War II.

No sooner had the dictatorial Franco succeeded in gaining absolute control of the country than he outlawed the expression of any views other than those of his right-wing, repressive, devoutly Catholic regime.

In the years after World War II, poverty and hunger were endemic throughout Spain, but in the 1950s American financial aid helped to boost economic growth. But even this modicum of prosperity did little to stem political protest. Indeed it was as an anti-Franco force that the militant terrorist organisation ETA (*Euskadi ta Askatasuna* – The Basque Country and Freedom) was formed in the 1950s. In 1973 an ETA bomb killed Admiral Luis Carrero Blanco, Franco's prime minister in Madrid. It became ever more obvious that repression could not be sustained. When Franco died on 20 November 1975, Spain was already in a psychological state of transition. The right realised that a return to democracy was inevitable; the left was ready to concede a restoration of the monarchy, and Juan Carlos I became king.

Emerging from Dictatorship

The country's first free general election in 40 years was held in 1977. Under the constitution that was subsequently passed Spain became not the single, indivisible entity to which Franco had always aspired but a country in which devolution was recognised as the only way forward. Spain was divided into a series of autonomous regions.

The Basque country in particular was given a great deal of independence to administer its own affairs, but this was not enough to satisfy hardline Basque nationalists who have continued their violent campaign against governments of both left- and right-wing persuasions.

Northwest Spain is an amalgam of autonomous regions – Navarra, La Rioja, the Basque country, Cantabria, Asturias, Galicia and the northern part of Castilla y León. Each of these enjoys its own particular character, with its own customs and cuisine, but all contribute to a modern Western country that is an integral part of the European Union.

Above: Franco the family man
Left: graffito of Basque resistance

HISTORY HIGHLIGHTS

800,000 BC *Homo erectus* is active in Sierra de Atapuerca near Burgos.

14,000 BC Paintings appear on cave walls at Altamira.

1,000 BC Celts settle in Galicia.

75 BC Pompey founds Pamplona.

61 BC Julius Caesar conquers Galicia.

26–19 BC Cantabrian War brings the last parts of Spain, Cantabria and Asturias under Roman dominion.

AD 476 Collapse of Rome. Visigoths take control of Spain and convert to Christianity.

711 Moors invade Spain and defeat Visigoths.

722 The Visigoth Pelayo defeats the Moors and establishes the kingdom of Asturias.

744 Christians under Alfonso I of Asturias capture León.

813 St James's tomb is (supposedly) discovered in Galicia.

866–910 Alfonso III (El Magno) moves Christian capital to León.

905 Navarra becomes a kingdom under Sancho I.

910–70 Fernán González wins autonomy from León for the county of Castile.

1000–35 Sancho the Great extends kingdom of Navarre.

1037 Fernando I of Castile seizes León and unites the two kingdoms.

1205 León Cathedral consecrated.

1406 Palace built for Carlos III of Navarre in Olite.

1469 Isabel of Castile weds Fernando of Aragón, uniting Catholic Spain.

1491 Birth of Ignatius Loyola, founder of the Jesuits.

1492 Moors expelled from Spain.

1512 Fernando annexes Navarra to complete Spain's unification.

1521 Juan Sebastián Elcano, a Basque, brings Magellan's round-the-world voyage home.

1540 Basque University founded at Oñati.

1588 Defeat of the Spanish Armada followed by English raids on Galicia.

1808–13 The War of Independence, or Peninsula War, follows Napoleon's invasion of Spain. French defeated with British support from Wellington's army.

1833–39 The First Carlist War between liberal supporters of Isabel and the conservative supporters (Carlists) of Fernando VIII's brother, Carlos.

1847–49 Second Carlist War.

1853–4 Famine in Galicia

1863 *Cantares Gallegos* by the poetess Rosalia de Castro is pivotal in a renaissance of the Galician language.

1872–76 Third Carlist War.

1894 Basque Nationalist Party (PNV) formed.

1931 Second Republic instituted. Alfonso XIII goes into exile.

1934 Revolt in Asturias. A rebellion of miners in Oviedo is quashed.

1936 Popular Front wins the General Election in February but General Franco and his co-conspirators launch a rebellion which sparks the Civil War.

1937 Franco's forces bomb Gernika.

1939 General Franco wins the war.

1941 Santander ravaged by fire.

1959 ETA, the Basque separatist group, is founded.

1975 Death of Franco. Accession of Juan Carlos I.

1977 First free elections in 40 years bring Socialists to power.

1979 Statute of autonomy introduced for Basque country.

1996 Socialists lose power to the right-of-centre Partido Popular.

1997 Bilbao Guggenheim Museum opens.

2002 Peseta replaced by Euro. North-western coastline suffers ecological disaster after oil tanker Prestige breaks up and sinks.

2003 Indefinite ban imposed on Basque separatist Batasuna party.

2004 Islamic terrorist bombs in Madrid kill 191 people. Socialist Party under Zapatero defies polls in a return to power.

2005 Voters approve the EU constitution in a referendum.

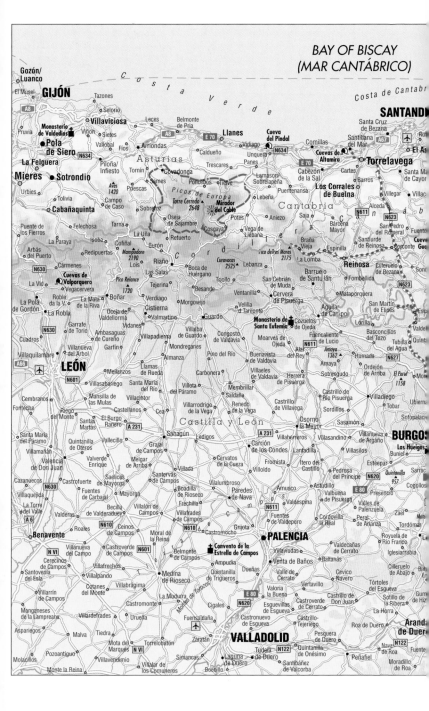

BAY OF BISCAY
(MAR CANTÁBRICO)

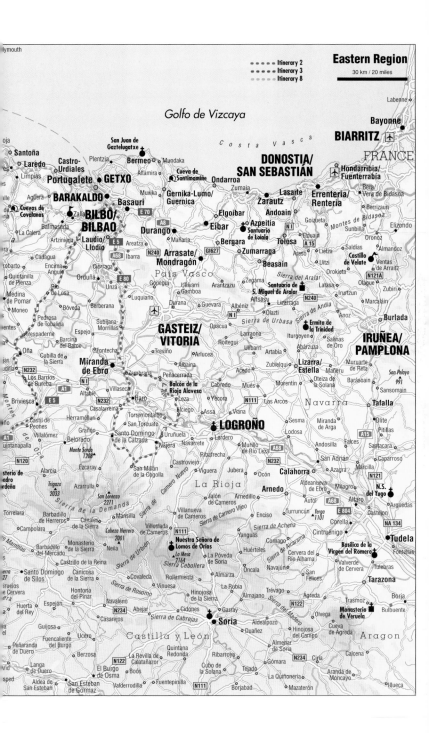

Eastern Region

····· Itinerary 2
····· Itinerary 3
····· Itinerary 8

30 km / 20 miles

Golfo de Vizcaya

C o s t a   V a s c a

Labenne

Bayonne

BIARRITZ

FRANCE

Plymouth

oja

Santoña
Laredo
Castro-
Urdiales
Limpias
Portugalete **GETXO**

San Juan de
Gaztelugatxe
Plentzia
Bermeo   Mundaka
Altamira
Cueva de
Santimamiñe
Muxika
Ondarroa
Zumaia

**DONOSTIA/
SAN SEBASTIÁN**

Hondarribia/
Fuenterrabía
Bera/
Vera de Bidasoa
Berriozar

BARAKALDO
Aguera
Cuevas de
Covalanas
Zalla
Balmaseda

Basauri
**BILBO/
BILBAO**
Laudio/
Llodio

Gernika-Lumo/
Guernica
Lasarte
Zarautz
Andoain
Errenteria/
Rentería
Goizueta
Elizondo
Oronoz
Almandoz

E70
A8
Durango
Mañaria
Elgoibar
Eibar
Azpeitia
Santuario
de Loiola
Bergara
N I
Elduain
Saldías
Lietza
Uitzi

Artziniega
La Calera
E5
Areatza
A68
Ibarra
N240
GI627
Zumarraga
Tolosa
A15
Orokieta
Uitzi
Orozko
Castillo
de Velate
Ventas
de Arraitz
N121A

Cadagua
Encima
Anguio
Orduña
Ciórraga
**Arrasate/
Mondragón**
Beasain
Areso
Olague
Zubiri

robarto
Quintanilla
de Pienza
E80
Unzá
País Vasco
Gopegui
Ulibarri
Gamboa
Arantzazu
Zegama
Santuario de
S. Miguel de Aralar
Altsasu
Lizarraga
N240
Latasa
Irurtzun
Marcalain

Medina
de Pomar
Moneo
Río
de Losa
Berberana
Luquiano
Durana
Guevara
Albéniz
Sierra del Aralar
Olazti
Sierra de Urbasa
Ermita de
la Trinidad
Salinas
de Oro
Anoz
Burlada
Zubiri

Pedrosa
de Tobalina
Trespaderne
Bóveda
Subijana-
Morillas
Opacua
Larraona
Roitegui
**IRUÑEA/
PAMPLONA**

Oña
Cubilla de
la Sierra
Fontecha
**GASTEIZ/
VITORIA**
Treviño
Albaina
Arlucea
Artabia
Zubielqui
Lizarra/
Estella
Oteiza de
la Solana
Muruarte
de Reta
Barásoain
San Pelayo
991

N232
Los Barrios
de Bureba
Miranda
de Ebro
N I
Zambrana
Peñacerrada
Acedo
Mues
Morentin
Mañeru
Sansomain

Briviesca
E5
Altable
Villaseca
N232
Haro
Balcón de la
Rioja Alavesa
Leza
Cabredo
Yécora
Assa
N111
Los Arcos
Navarra
Tafalla

Castil de
Peones
Villalómez
A1
Casalarreina
Torremontalbo
San Torcuato
Elciego
Viana
Sesma
Miranda
de Arga
Olite
Pitillas

riño
Herramélluri
Grañón
Santo Domingo
de la Calzada
Uruñuela
Lardero
Lodosa
A15
A1
Belorado
Monte Sordo
1206
Nájera
Navarrete
Munilo
de Río Leza
A68
Andosilla
Falces
Caparroso

N120
Alarcia
Ezcaray
Ribafrecha
Jubera
N232
Calahorra
San Adrián
Azagra
Marcilla
N111

sterio de
edro
deña
Trigaza
2033
Azarrulla
San Millán
de la Cogolla
Castroviejo
Viguera
Ocón
Aldeanueva
de Ebro
Milagro
N.S.
del Yugo
Arguedas

Torrelara
Barbadillo
de Herreros
Sierra de la Demanda
San Lorenzo
2271
Mansilla
Villanueva
de Cameros
Jalón de
Cameros
Arnedillo
Arnedo
Autol
A68
Alfaro
Corella
NA134

Campolara
Barbadillo
del Mercado
Monasterio
de la Sierra
Neila
Cabezo Herrero
2001
Villoslada
de Cameros
N111
Enciso
Turruncún
Yerga
1101
E804
Castejón

s Mambas
Santo Domingo
de Silos
Castillo de
la Reina
Canicosa
de la Sierra
**Nuestra Señora de
Lomos de Orios**
*La Mesa
2164
Sierra Cebollera*
La Póveda
de Soria
Yanguas
Cornago
Sierra de Alcarama
Cervera del
Río Alhama
Valverde de
Cervera
Basílica de la
Virgen del Romero
Fontellas
Tudela
Tulebras

erra
27
ruelos
era
Huerta
del Rey
Espejón
Hontoria
del Pinar
Navaleno
Sierra de Rosomo
Covaleda
Vinuesa
Rollamienta
Almarza
Huérteles
Navajún
San
Felices
Trévago
Agreda
Trasmoz
Borja
Monasterio
de Veruela
Bulbuente

Sierra de Urbión
N234
Abejar
Cidones
Sierra de Cabrejas
Garray
Almajano
Oncala
La Rubia
Sierra del Madero
N122
Olvega
Cueva
de Agreda
Aragon

el
Peñaranda
de Duero
Fuencaliente
del Burgo
Berzosa
Ucero
Castilla y León
Quintana
Redonda
Ribarroya
Aldealpozo
Hinojosa
del Campo
Almenar
de Soria
Cirla
Calcena

Vid
sped
Langa
de Duero
Aldea de
San Esteban
El Burgo
de Osma
San Esteban
de Gormaz
N122
La Revilla de
Calatañazor
Boós
Valderrodilla
N111
Fuentepinilla
Calatañazor
Soria
Duañes
Cubo de
la Solana
Tejado
Gómara
Borjabad
Mazaterón
N234
La Quiñoneria
Illueca
Aranda de
Moncayo

the Basque Country

Bilbao is the principal port of the Basque country, a region bordering the Bay of Biscay that covers parts of northern Spain and southwest France. The Basque country incorporates seven provinces but is defined more by people and language than by geographical boundaries. Three of the provinces are in France, three – Bizkaia (Vizcaya), Gipuzkoa (Guipúzcoa) and Alava – constitute the País Vasco, an autonomous region of Spain, and the seventh province, Navarra, is only partially Basque.

Constitutionally the Spanish Basque country enjoys a significant measure of self-government, including its own police force, though numerous Basques want the full independence of their own state, and a significant minority support the violent activities of the terrorist organisation ETA. As a traveller in the region you are unlikely to see many signs of political extremism, but you will frequently see the red, white and green *ikurriña* Basque flag.

The Basque urge towards separatism is understandable. They are not a Spanish people and are clearly different from their neighbours along the Cantabrian coast, in the central Pyrenees, and to the south in Castile. Moreover, the Basques can claim to be the oldest race in Europe.

They are particularly proud of a culinary tradition that is rich in more senses than one. Indeed the Basque country is considered to have the country's most sophisticated cuisine – locals frequently meet to cook together in gastronomic societies. Basques, especially the men, also identify closely with age-old traditional local sports such as pelota (in which two players hit a ball against a wall), agrarian feats of strength, and regattas.

Basques call their country Euskadi and their language, Euskera. The use of this ancient language, which appears to be related to no other tongue, was suppressed by Franco but is now widespread. Many street and other public signs are in both Euskera and Spanish – don't be surprised to find the Spanish text crossed out by separatists making a political point – or in Euskera only. Many of the region's towns and cities are known by both their Spanish and Euskera names: San Sebastián is also Donostia, Pamplona is Iruña and so on. This book uses the Basque name for preference and gives the Spanish version in brackets, or vice versa for internationally known cities and for places that are referred to by their Spanish name.

Although you will impress the locals by using Basque names, be warned that the Basque country is not a homogeneous society: there are a great many Basques who do not speak Euskera, as well as people from other parts of Spain who are resident in the region but to whom the local language is an unnecessary complication to life.

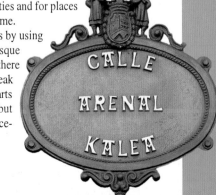

Left: taking a break in Bilbao
Right: a bilingual street sign

1. BILBAO *(see map below)*

A day's stroll around the city centre, covering the old town (Casco Viejo) in the morning and the Museo Guggenheim by late afternoon. If you have time at the end of the day, take a bus or local train to Portugalete at the mouth of the river and walk across the unusual Puente Colgante bridge.

The starting point, the tourist information office on Paseo de Arenal, can be reached by a variety of buses or by a metro to Casco Viejo station. Note: directions use Spanish names – many street names in Bilbao are in both Spanish and Basque.

From the tourist information office, cross the small triangular park in front of you by the main path, with the Art Nouveau bandstand (complete with stained-glass roof) to your right. Cross the road and carry straight on (slightly to your left) down Calle del Correo. The first turn left off this street brings you into **Plaza Nueva**. This arcaded square, which dates back to 1830, is surrounded by lively bars and constitutes the heart of old Bilbao.

Cross the square diagonally and exit it beside **Café Bilbao**. This is a good place for tapas, as is the adjacent **Víctor Montes**. Turn left immediately to enter **Plaza de Unamuno**, a square at the base of a long flight of steps, named after the Bilbao-born writer Miguel de Unamuno (1864–1936). Cross this square diagonally, keeping right, and head down Calle María Muñoz to visit the **Euskal Museoa** (**Basque Museum**; Tue–Sat 11am–5pm; Sun 11am–2pm),

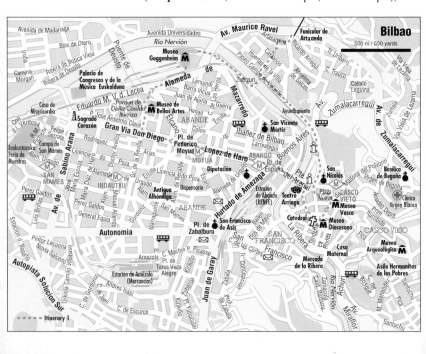

basque country

which has exhibits on Basque archaeology and history. One highlight here is the Idolo de Mikeldi, an odd pre-Christian sculpture of an animal.

After visiting the museum head back to Plaza de Unamuno and take the road on the other side of the museum, Calle de la Cruz, passing the **Iglesia de Santos Juanes** church on your left. Fork right at the grey fountain-cum-bench and you are in Calle de la Tendería. This is one of the so-called **Siete Calles**, the original Seven Streets around which Bilbao was built. Today this neighbourhood has a reputation for being a good area for a pub crawl.

Pilgrim Stop
Tendería leads you to the asymmetrical porch of the **Catedral de Santiago**, built to serve pilgrims on their way to Santiago de Compostela. Cross the porch to reach the Plazuela Santiago and the main door of a building that combines Gothic with neo-Gothic elements. In 2000 it was reopened after a long period of closure, though not as long as the renovation work, which has been going on since the end of the 14th century. The cloister is particularly worth seeing – ask in the sacristy if it is locked.

Leave the Plazuela Santiago on Calle Bidebarrieta. This brings you to the handsome, neo-baroque **Teatro Arriaga** (tel: 944 310 310), which stands at the end of the Puente del Arenal bridge. Subscribers who could not make it to the opening night in 1890 listened to the inaugural opera over the telephone. The Arriaga was burnt down in 1915 and was rebuilt four years' later. It now stages theatre, dance, opera and classical-music concerts. If you want to cut down on the walking, catch a bus from the stop opposite the theatre and get off after Plaza Moyúa.

Crossing the bridge over the Ría del Nervion (also known as Ría Ibaizabal), leaving the Casco Viejo behind, you enter **The Ensanche**, the focus of city expansion in the 19th and 20th centuries. On your left is the green and yellow facade of the **Estación de Santander**. This French-influenced evocation of the railway age, one of the city's six train stations, dates back to 1898.

Two British Influences
A few steps beyond the end of the bridge, a covered alley to your left takes you to the door of **La Sociedad Bilbaina**, an exclusive social club that was modelled on the clubs of London – evidence of Bilbao's long relationship with the UK. At the end of the short street leading up hill from the bridge you reach the **Plaza Circular**, dominated by a statue of Diego López de Haro who founded the city of Bilbao in 1300. The striking metal-and-glass metro station entrances in the square show how Bilbao has kept up with the times. They were designed by the British architect Sir Norman Foster and have been affectionately dubbed *fosteritos* by commuters. Also on the Plaza Circular is the **Café La Granja**, which has changed little since it opened in 1926.

Above Left: welcome to Café Víctor Montes
Above: tombstone outside the Museo Vasco

From the Plaza Circular walk up the Gran Vía de Don Diego López de Haro, Bilbao's principal street. Many of the city's smartest shops are on or near this great artery, beginning with the **Corte Inglés** department store. There are also a great many bars and restaurants. The **Café Iruña** (corner of Colón de Larreátegui and Berástegui, tel: 94 423 70 21), a *belle époque* neo-Mudejar fantasy, is a popular meeting place and also serves a good *menu del día* at a reasonable price. **La Taberna de los Mundos** (Simón Bolívar 17, tel: 94 441 35 23) has won prizes for its sandwiches. If you want to splash out, **Guria** (Gran Vía 66, tel: 94 441 90 13) serves traditional Basque food and **Serantes** (Licenciado Poza 16, tel: 94 421 21 29) excels at fish and shellfish.

Contrasting Art Museums

On the left as you make your way up the Gran Vía, you pass the eclectically ornamented facade of the **Palacio de la Diputación Foral** (No 25), built in 1900, at the height of Bilbao's commercial and industrial prowess, as a seat for Bizkaia's provincial government. Cross the elliptical Plaza Moyúa (on which stands the Carlton, the city's leading hotel) and continue along Gran Vía. Turn right at Alameda Conde de Arteche. To your right is the large **Parque de Doña Casilda de Iturrizar**, in front of which is the **Museo de Bellas Artes** (www.museobilbao.com; Tue–Sat 10am–8pm; Sun 10am–2pm), featuring an excellent collection of Basque and Spanish art – Velázquez, Zurbarán, El Greco, Goya and Picasso – that spans the centuries, by contrast with its insistently contemporary cousin, the Guggenheim.

Continuing in the same direction, take the path between the Fine Arts Museum and the park and you come to a busy road junction. Cross this towards the Shell petrol station

Above: the titanium-coated Museo Guggenheim
Right: Jeff Koons's gigantic flowery dog sculpture

and you will be on the Alameda de Mazarredo. Walk down this road, crossing it where you can, to reach the attraction around which this formerly commercial and industrial city recently reinvented itself. You can't miss the **Museo Guggenheim** (www.guggenheim-bilbao.es, Tue–Sun 10am–8pm) – it's just beyond a gigantic flowery dog sculpture by Jeff Koons. The innovative titanium-coated Guggenheim building by Frank O. Gehry is worth seeing from all angles. Often less worthy is the quality of art exhibited inside. Given that the entrance price is relatively expensive, you might want to give it a miss, unless you are particularly interested in the exhibition currently on show.

Leave the museum by the exit next to the shop and ATM machines, which will bring you on to a terrace beside the river. Turn right and follow the broad footpath to cross Santiago Calatrava's white footbridge, the **Zubizuri**. If you have time for a detour, turn left on the other side of the bridge, cross the road and head up Múgica y Butrón to reach the start of the **Artxanda funicular railway**, from the top of which there is a panoramic view of the city. Otherwise, turn right at the end of the bridge and proceed on the other bank past the **ayuntamiento** (town hall) on your left. This stiff and sober building is said to reflect the mercantile manner of Bilbainos. Pass the Bizkaibus bus station on your right and you will arrive at the rear of the tourist information office from which this itinerary started. You might now be ready to plunge into the Casco Viejo again for tapas or an early dinner.

2. LA RIOJA *(see map, p18–19)*

An overnight trip to the vineyards and bodegas of La Rioja, a region that also features a wealth of monasteries, churches and handsome towns.

Start in Haro, south of Bilbao. On the A68 toll motorway follow the signs for Burgos and Logroño and take the Logroño–Zaragoza fork. Turn off at exit 9, the first after the Río Ebro. Less directly, you can take the N240 road via Vitoria. Visits to bodegas *should be booked in advance: consult the tourist office, either in Haro (tel: 941 30 33 66, www.beronia.com), in Laguardia (tel: 945 60 08 45, www.laguardia-alava.com), or La Rioja Turismo (tel: 941 29 12 60, www.lariojaturismo.com)*

Haro, the wine capital of La Rioja, has some lovely old buildings in the streets around its main square, the **Plaza de la Paz**, but the main reason to visit the town is to see the wineries. The tourist office on Plaza San Agustin will tell you which ones are open to the public and when. The safest bets are Bodegas Muga on weekdays and Bodegas Bilbainas at weekends. There is also a **Museo del Vino** (Wine Museum; Mon–Sat 10am–2pm and 4–8pm; Sun mornings only) where you can find out

Right: depiction of La Rioja's leading industry

how La Rioja turned its local grape, tempranillo, into an international best-seller. For a suitable base try **Los Agustinos** (Calle San Agustin, tel: 941 3113 08), a 14th-century convent converted into a hotel. Haro may seem like a haven of tranquillity but on 29 June its people stage a **Batalla del Vino**, a free-for-all fight with wine as ammunition, on a hill outside the town.

Leave Haro via the Avenida Santo Domingo, the road on which you arrived, which passes the bullring and Bodegas Paternina, another famous name of La Rioja wine. Keep straight when this road becomes the N126 motorway then the LR111 to the **Santo Domingo de la Calzada** shrine on the road to Santiago de Compostela. Park on the road surrounding the old town and walk on the pedestrianised streets. You can glimpse the interior of the **cathedral** (Mon–Sat 10am–6.30pm) from the door on the square , but it is better to go around to the entrance on Calle del Cristo and pay the admission price. (On the square is a state-run hotel and restaurant – the Parador; tel: 941 34 03 00.)

In the cathedral it is impossible not to notice two chickens kept in an ornate cage. Tourists are delighted when one of them crows because it reminds them of the reason for the chickens' presence. According to a popular legend that dates back to the 11th century, a young pilgrim was passing through Santo Domingo de la Calzada when he was wrongly accused of theft and hanged. His parents found him still alive on the gallows some time later. 'St Dominic has saved my life,' he told them. They reported this miracle to the local *corregidor* (chief magistrate) who was having lunch. The judge scoffed, saying that their son was no more alive than the roast chickens he was about to eat, whereupon the cock and hen stood up on his plate and crowed.

From Santo Domingo a well-signposted road takes off in the direction of San Millán de la Cogolla. This road passes through the town of Berceo, 12th-century birthplace of Gonzalo de Berceo, the first poet to write in the dialect that would evolve into Spanish. Inspired like a true *riojano*, he wrote:

'I seek to write prose in the speech of the labourer
which the people use to speak with their neighbour
as I am not gifted enough to write another Latin rhyme
I think it will help to have a good glass of wine.'

The Great Monasteries

Soon after Berceo you come to **San Millán**, site of two monasteries. The older, smaller and more delightful of these, **Monasterio de Suso** (Tue–Sun 10am–1.30pm, 4–6pm. Maximum 25 people at a time. Access to the monastery only by micro-bus) is situated high up a winding road above the town. It was built in Mozarabic style between the 6th and 11th centuries.

Above: at the Santo Domingo de la Calzada shrine

The larger **Monasterio de Yuso** was founded in the valley below in the 11th century but most of what you see dates from the 16th–18th century. To visit Monasterio de Yuso you have to join one of the guided tours (between the hours of 10am–1.30pm and 4–6.30pm). The main features to look out for in the monastery church are the 17th-century gold altarpiece showing San Millán (St Emilian, 473–574), the Plateresque arch and the dark walnut pulpit. Upstairs you should look out for a facsimile of a 10th-century manuscript on which a monk scrawled notes in the margin. These are the first written examples of the Spanish and Basque languages. Attached to the Monasterio de Yuso is a *hostería* (4 star hotel, tel: 941 37 32 77); which provides both accommodation and meals.

From Yuso head back down the valley to Berceo, pass through the village and turn right on the LR205 for **Nájera**. Follow this road to the T-junction, and then turn left on the LR113 for Logroño and Nájera. When you get to Nájera, follow signs *to 'centro ciudad'* and *'conjunto histórico'*. Park near the river to explore the old town, which cowers beneath the red cliffs of Peña Malpica. Here stands the monastery of **Santa María la Réal** (Tue–Sat 9.30am–1pm, 4–7pm; Sun 10am–12.30pm, 4–6.30pm). The cloister is decorated with Plateresque tracery in unusual designs. Nájera was once the capital of the kingdom of Navarra, and the church of Santa María contains the royal pantheon of Navarra's kings from the 10th, 11th and 12th centuries. The tombs are 16th century. Also worth seeing are the Gothic choir stalls upstairs.

La Rioja Alavesa

The way out of Nájera is somewhat complicated. Start by following the signs for *'todas direcciones'* ('all routes') and you soon find your way on to the LR113 towards Cenicero via Uruñuela. Pass over the top of the main Burgos-Logroño road and head towards a range of mountains. A few kilometres later you pass over the top of the Bilbao–Logroño motorway. Drive through Cenicero and, on the way out, the Marques de Cáceres *bodega* is on your left.

Turn left on the LR211 for Laguardia and pass the Berberana bodega on your left. Cross the river and you are in Alava, one of the three Basque provinces. Here the road's map number changes, and some names now appear in Euskera (Basque). You are still in the La Rioja wine area; this part is called the Rioja Alavesa. Go straight on through Elciego, passing (on the left) the bodega of Marques de Riscal. This bodega has commissioned its own mini-Guggenheim, as a

Above: the Monasterio de Yuso
Right: in a celebratory mood

new headquarters, from Frank O. Gehry, which is due to be completed in 2005 and will include a hotel.

In front of you on a flat hilltop you will see the walled wine town of **Laguardia** (Basque name: Biasteri). Look out for the Iglesia de Santa María de los Reyes, which features the country's only perfectly preserved 14th-century polychrome Gothic portal, which is protected by a Renaissance facade. Not far from Laguardia is the **La Hoya prehistoric settlement**, which includes a museum full of archaeological discoveries and, at Elvillar, the La Chabola de la Hechicera dolmen.

From Laguardia take the A124 towards Vitoria. Turn right after the hospital on to the A2124 in the direction of Peñacerrada and Vitoria. The road winds up the side of rocky mountains to the **Balcón de la Rioja Alavesa** on the left. From here there is an expansive view of the plains, vineyards and towns below. Pass over the unspectacular 1,100-metre (3,600ft) Puerto de Herrera and begin a gradual descent. Turn left at the crossroads entrance to Peñacerrada, onto the A3126 via Zambrana to join the motorway back to Bilbao. Or continue to Vitoria, following signs for Bilbao via the N240.

3. THE BACK ROAD TO BURGOS *(see map, p18–19)*

Drive through the mountains and central plateau to the city of Burgos.

For this leisurely, scenic, two-day route, fill up with petrol as there are long stretches without a service station. Alternatively, you can visit Burgos in a day from Bilbao via the toll motorway (A68 to Miranda de Ebro then the A1).

Leave Bilbao along Calle Autonomía. Immediately after the road bends to the right, turn off left for Balmaseda on the BI636. Take a left turn onto the BI636 proper after passing under the flyover. In Sodupe, turn left over the railway line and river towards Artziniega (on the BI2604, which becomes the A2604). Drive up a valley and enter the province of Alava just before Artziniega. Circumscribe Artziniega following the signs for Trespaderne, still on the A2604. Shortly afterwards you enter Burgos province and the road changes number for a second time, to become the BU550. It climbs steadily and passes through a tunnel to emerge in the upland Valle de Losa.

Medieval Oña

In the middle of Trespaderne turn left on to the N629, through a gorge of the Ebro, and left again at a junction with the N232 (towards Logroño and Burgos). After another gorge you reach **Oña**, a suitable town in which to stretch your legs. Although somewhat dozy now, this was an important place in the Middle Ages, as indicated by the imposing Monasterio de San Salvador, now a hospital, at the centre of town, is evidence. The adjoining church contains a royal pantheon dedicated to the kingdoms of Navarra and Castile.

Rejoin the road to Logroño but take a right turn at Cornudilla for Briviesca

Above: the wine town of Laguardia

basque country

and Burgos. You are now on the dry plains of old Castile. **Briviesca** is a messy town but if you do stop here, check out the arcaded *plaza mayor* (main square), the Colegiata de Santa María, which has a Renaissance facade, and the Convento de Santa Clara, featuring a Renaissance altarpiece. For the journey from here to Burgos take the slow main road or a 35-km (22-mile) stretch of fast (toll) motorway. South of the motorway is the inconspicuous Sierra de Atapuerca, site of the oldest human remains found in Europe.

Franco's Capital

A stout, conservative city on the pilgrims' route known as the Road to Santiago de Compostela, **Burgos** was the capital of the kingdom of Castile and León from the mid 11th century until Spain's unification in 1492. More recently it served as Franco's capital during the Civil War. Today it features three great

monuments, each of which is worth a visit, and a host of smaller ones that you should see if you have the time. The Gothic **cathedral** (Mon–Sat 9.30am–1pm and 4–7pm; Sun 9.30–11.45am and 4–7pm) is the main point of interest in the city centre. It is the third largest cathedral in Spain (after those in Seville and Toledo).

In the middle of the cathedral is the tomb of El Cid. Born Rodrigo Díaz in 1043, he is better known by his honorary name, which derives from the Arabic for 'lord'. As a result of the anonymous 12th-century poem *El Cantar del Mío Cid*, he became the hero of the Christian Reconquest which saw the Moors driven out of the country. The truth is somewhat different: in the course of his life El Cid fought for both the Christians and the Muslims. Standing by his tomb, look up to see an extraordinary vaulting of the lantern which King Felipe III thought 'more likely made by angels than by men'. The other most noteworthy feature is the ornate Capilla de los Condestables (Constables' Chapel) behind the altar.

Opposite the cathedral is the Mesón del Cid hotel and restaurant (tel: 947 20 87 15). If you are hungry, there are lots of restaurants clustered around the cathedral, but if you want to avoid crowds of tourists, especially in summer, walk past the square to the other end of town. At the end of Puente de San Pablo, in the neighbourhood around an equestrian statue of El Cid, are several other possibilities. For instance, La Posada (Plaza Santo Domingo de Guzmán, 18; tel: 947 20 45 78) does a hearty *menu del día* and also plates of rich Castilian meats.

Above: the Gothic cathedral of Burgos
Right: equestrian statue of El Cid

There are two other major attractions in Burgos: the monastery and a convent, but unfortunately they are not only a considerable distance from the city centre but also in opposite directions. The church of the **Cartuja de Miraflores** monastery (Mon–Sat 10.15am–3pm and 4–6pm; Sun 11.15am–3pm) stands in peaceful surroundings 3.5km (2 miles) to the east. In marked contrast to its bare stone walls is a huge golden altarpiece created by the local 15th-century sculptor Gil de Siloé.

The **Réal Monasterio de Las Huelgas** (Tue–Sat 10am–1.15pm, 4.30–5.45pm; Sun 10am–2.15pm) is, despite its name, a convent not a monastery. This is, at 1.5km (1 mile) away, at least nearer the centre. More commercial and busier than Miraflores, and still exuding the wealth, power and influence it historically enjoyed, it combines Romanesque, Gothic and Mudejar elements.

Around the Embalse del Ebro

Leave Burgos on the N623/627 for Santander across the plains to the north. After Ubierna turn off for Santander on the N623. The ensuing few kilometres take you over two inconspicuous passes and through drab moorland scenery which can, on a bad day, be somewhat bleak and lonely.

Shortly after Tubilla you enter a long gorge of cliffs, pillars and arches. If you are not in a hurry to get to the coast, turn off at Quintanilla for a detour to **Orbaneja del Castillo**, a village deep in the gorge where there are a couple of guest houses and a bar from which you can watch vultures. Beyond it – further off the main route – is the Romanesque church of **San Martín de Elines** and the cave-churches of **Arroyuelos** and **Cadarso**.

Staying on the main road, however, you climb out of the gorge and set off across more wild, unpopulated moorland. The trees and pastures of the green north begin over the 1,000 metre- (3,280ft-) high Puerto de Carrales. You now skirt past the **Embalse del Ebro**, a great reservoir held back by a tiny dam: sprawling but shallow, it is home to more than 50 species of birds, many of them resident all year round. The lake perimeter is an area worth exploring if you have at least another day to spare. If so, it's a good idea to stay in **Reinosa**: one of several recommended stopover options here is the inexpensive Villa Rosa (tel: 942 75 47 47; www.villarosa.com), which is both delightful and homely. A one-way road from there takes you up to

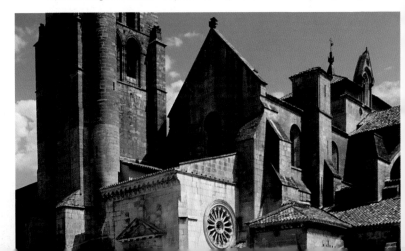

basque country

the **Pico de Tres Mares** from which there is a view of the Picos de Europa *(see page 50)*.

From the reservoir shore the road climbs to another pass, the Puerto del Escudo, and begins a long, steep descent towards the lowlands of Cantabria. Just before San Vicente de Toranzo, keep an eye open for the Posada del Pas (tel: 942 59 44 11), which provides good, medium-priced accommodation.

Puente Viesgo, 4km (2½ miles) south of Torrelavega, is known for its baths, salmon fishing and, said to predate even those at Altamira, the palaeolithic Cueva del Castillo cave paintings at Monte Castillo above the town. Once in the town turn right towards Bilbao or head on for Santander. Alternatively, and especially if you are looking for some classy accommodation, head for Santillana del Mar *(see Itinerary 8, page 48)*, following signs for Torrelavega. Drive past Torrelavega and take exit 234 onto the S480 for Santillana del Mar. Follow the signs to the railway and river, which you cross at Puente San Miguel. Passing the turn-off for the caves of Altamira on your left, you will find yourself at the approach to Santillana del Mar.

4. THE COAST OF BIZKAIA *(see map, p32)*

This route explores the pretty fishing ports and developing holiday resorts that line the indented coast of Bizkaia, one of the most attractive regions of northwest Spain, and within easy distance of Bilbao.

Without any stops, this itinerary can be done in a long morning, returning to Bilbao for lunch, but a day trip is probably a better option. In good weather, take swimming gear, and possibly a pair of binoculars.

From the centre of Bilbao, cross the bridge by the Guggenheim Museum (Puente Principes de España, also known as Puente de la Salve) and follow the road around to your right. After the Parque Etxebarria, turn off right towards Bermeo, just before a tunnel. Turn left to pass the **Basilíca de Begoña** (where the Virgin Mary is said to have appeared, and which is named after the province's patron saint, the Virgin of Begoña) and left at the T-junction, still for Bermeo (on the BI631). You feed into a dual

Left: Réal Monasterio de Las Huelgas. **Above:** Pico de Tres Mares. **Right:** Urdaibai Reserve

carriageway that, beyond Mungia, eventually leads to a roundabout. Turn left here for Bakio and Bermeo. After Meñaka turn left on the BI3101 for Bakio.

Bakio is a pleasant fishing village with fine beaches but it is hardly an essential stop. Instead, turn off as soon as you arrive and head up some wooded slopes towards Bermeo. When you emerge from the trees you will

have good views over the Basque coast. Keep a sharp look out for a left turn to San Juanera Urizarretatik and the reasonably priced Eneperi restaurant (tel: 94 619 40 65).

Raided by Sir Francis Drake

Commencing next to the restaurant, a footpath descends to **San Juan de Gaztelugatxe**, a chapel perched on a crag high above the waves, and reached from the shore by the steps of an attractive walled, cobbled causeway over the rocks. Sir Francis Drake is said to have attacked the chapel, purloined the valuables and tossed the resident hermit into the sea. If you don't want to visit the chapel but are content with just a view of it, walk down the lane past the restaurant – but be warned, it does become very steep – until you come to a sharp, left-hand bend. If you prefer to drive down, carry on along the coast road until, on the left, you see a car park furnished with three brown benches. From here a twisting road (marked by a sign prohibiting buses) drops down to a turning circle at the start of the causeway. Another warning: the quality of the road is, in some places, terrible so you might want to park halfway down.

Continue along the coast road past the lighthouse and enter the **Urdaibai Nature Reserve** of the Ría de Gernika, a UNESCO-designated area where nature and traditional human activities such as farming and fishing are supposed to interact in harmony. The next town along the route, **Bermeo**, was once Bilbao's rival port. Though smaller than its conurbation neighbour, it is a sizeable fishing port specialising in white tuna. When the fleet is in, the harbour is a pretty sight. The Torre de Ercilla near the port contains the **Museo del Pescador** (Fishing Museum: Tue–Sat 10am–1.30pm, 4–7.30pm, Sun morning only), where you can learn all about the whaling that was once a vital Basque industry. The town's official seal features a spouting whale.

The Prettiest Town

If you stop nowhere else along the coast, take a stroll through the pretty town of **Mundaka**, which has excellent surfing beaches. Either park on the outskirts or navigate narrow streets lined with houses notable for their glassed-in wooden galleries and find a parking space on the square near the harbour and tourist office. If you're looking for a place to stay, the Hotel Atalaya (Calle Itxaropen, tel: 964 17 70 00) is an especially pleasant option.

Once you are through with Mundaka, return to the road heading towards Gernika. Just after the tight bend, on the left there is a viewpoint over the sandflats and beaches of the Ría de Gernika. From here to Gernika the road has been built up with holiday homes but you can still catch the occasional glimpse of the water on your left. Most of the signposts directed towards points of interest are written in Euskera only.

Gernika-Lumo (Guernica) is a rather bewildering town, its historical significance not at all obvious. The town's claim to fame derives from Picasso's gigantic, propagandist Civil War painting, which now hangs in the Museo Reina Sofía in Madrid. Picasso created his painting in response to an atrocity that shocked the world. At 4.40pm on 26 April 1937, the German Condor Legion's warplanes, fighting on behalf of Franco's rebel forces, bombed the town. It was market day: the streets were packed with civilians – farmers, stallholders, customers, and refugees – and there were no air defences to protect them from what was effectively a dress rehearsal for the saturation bombing raids of World War II. Gernika might well have been specifically targeted for the air raid because of its significance to the Basques – the town has symbolised Basque autonomy since the 14th century.

Above Left: ship repairs in Bermeo
Right: the Tree of Gernika

The Tree of Gernika

At the top of the town you will find the neo-classical **Casa de Juntas** (10am–2pm and 4–6pm), which dates to the 19th-century. Have a look around the grounds before you enter. The remnant of a tree trunk known as the 'Old Tree' is a specimen of the oak tree venerated as a symbol of Basque freedom. Behind the Casa de Juntas is the Tree of Gernika, not far from which stands a sapling that will one day replace it. For centuries, the parliament of Bizkaia, the General Assemblies, met under the Tree of Gernika. Here, too, the ruler of Spain would swear to observe the Basques' own laws (*fueros*). In 1876, however, the General Assemblies were suspended and the *fueros* abolished. Only in 1979 did the Basques win a measure of autonomy that returned the Assembly Chamber in the Casa de Juntas to its proper purpose. The glass ceiling of the neighbouring Stained Glass Room depicts the Tree of Gernika, the economic activities of the Basques and, round the edges, the most important monuments of Bizkaia.

Next to the Casa, the **Parque de los Pueblos de Europa** is divided into the Basques' four ecosystems – beech, oak and holm oak, woodland, and wetlands. Check out the sculptures by Eduardo Chillida and Henry Moore.

If you have the time for a lengthy detour from Gernika, take the road towards Lekeitio. On the right, after about 4km (2½ miles), you will see a right turning to **La Cueva de Santimamiñe**. The chamber with prehistoric paintings, for which Santimamiñe is famous, is closed to the public but you can see the other caves (visits Mon–Fri at 10am, 11.15am, 12.30pm, 4.30pm and 6pm). If you're hungry, a good and convenient option is the reasonably priced Lezika restaurant (tel: 94 625 29 75) beside the caves.

Opposite the restaurant a track marked 'Acceso único al Bosque Pintado de Iberrola' leads to the Bosque de Oma, a steep slope with a large group of pine trees whose trunks have been painted by the local artist Agustín Ibarrola in a number of fascinating ways. Some of the markings align from particular viewpoints to create trompe l'oeil illusions of, for instance, a gigantic eye, and a zig-zag. Allow up to two hours to walk to and from the 'painted wood'. Then return to Gernika and follow directions back to Bilbao. Just before Amorebieta join the N634 for Bilbao and either stay on this road or take the faster (toll fee) motorway.

5. SAN SEBASTIAN *(see maps, p32 & 36)*

San Sebastián (Donostia) has been a fashionable resort since Queen Isabel II came to bathe in the sea in 1845. This itinerary can be completed in a morning but a full day gives you time to visit the museums.

Coming from out of town, follow signs to Centro Ciudad from the A8 motorway; you should be following the left bank of the Río Urumea on Paseo del Arbol de Guernica. There is an underground car park beneath Reina Regente, where this itinerary starts.

Begin at the tourist information office on the corner of Reina Regente (near the end of Puente de la Zurriola). Facing the river, turn right and walk along Paseo de la República Argentina, past

the rear of the **María Cristina**, which stands out, not only as the city's finest hotel but as an evocative reminder of the *belle époque*'s sybaritic spirit.

Cross the **Puente María Cristina** – San Sebastián's prettiest or ugliest bridge, depending on how you look at it. Four cream-coloured pavilions guard its ramparts and the bridge itself is decorated with sculpted black-ironwork dragons, sea monsters and anchors.

Turn left at the end of the bridge and walk down the other bank of the river – the more pleasant, less busy side. The roof of the **railway station** that runs parallel with the embankment was designed by Gustave Eiffel. Cross the Puente de la Zurriola and turn right into the Paseo de Salamanca, which soon becomes the Paseo Nuevo. There is usually a sea breeze blowing down this

paseo and, on the other side of the coastal wall, waves crash on to large, square-cut boulders. As you round the corner of the headland you see Monte Igueldo, crowned by a gigantic statue of Christ, ahead. Continuing along Paseo Nuevo, you have a view of Isla Santa Clara, an islet in the mouth of

Above Left: the Assembly Chamber's Stained Glass Room. **Left:** the 'painted wood'
Above: looking out to sea on the promenade of La Concha beach

basque country

the bay that can, in summer, be reached by a ferry service from the harbour.

Monte Urgull

When the *paseo* heads towards the mainland again take the ramp that leads to the summit of Monte Urgull, and a municipal park (summer: 8am–9pm, winter: 8am–7pm). Don't be surprised if you get lost exploring the paths around the hill – none of the maps of the area are very accurate. As a general guide, head for the summit then come down on the city-side: this way you should not have a problem reaching the harbour, from which you can get your bearings.

Follow the ramp upwards. Just to the right of the first fork is the **English Cemetery** (Cementerio de los Ingleses), which dates from 1835–37. Here lie the fallen soldiers of an English military contingent, commanded by General Sir Lacy Evans, that was sent to defend the liberal-leaning San Sebastián against Carlist aggression. The cemetery is now in a lamentable condition; the main tomb has been defaced and its statuary knocked down.

Look for an ascending zig-zag path on the road's other fork, which leads to a narrow arched passage. Pass through the passage, turn right up a broad flight of steps and you enter the fortress of **Castillo de la Mota**. From the battlements of the castle, above which the Christ statue reaches for the sky, there are splendid views of La Concha, old town rooftops , the harbour, and Monte Igeldo across the water. Turn right at the base of the castle steps

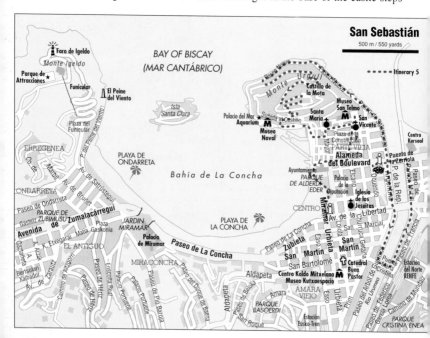

towards the **Batería de Santiago**, one of several gun emplacements that kept a watch over the bay, but that now commands little other than a fine view.

The following part of the itinerary involves walking down lots of steps. For an easier descent follow signs to the 'Muelle' (harbour). A sign to Batería de las Damas masks a flight of hidden steps. Descend these steps, passing through the arch, and you emerge on the terrace of a café. Bear right and down another hidden flight of steps. You will eventually arrive at a road, on which you can turn left towards the city. You are now at the **Batería de las Damas**, where a row of six immobile field guns sit stranded, high above the port. Turn right down a long flight of steps with a metal handrail. At the bottom turn right above the harbour and rooftops. Descend the ramp and the staircase from the pedestrian square to the **Aquarium** (winter: 10am–8pm, summer: 10am–10pm), whose glass tunnel affords a view of the sealife all around you.

Two Museums, Two Churches

After the aquarium descend the steps in front of the entrance, as far as the harbour level, and walk round the harbour towards the city. You will pass the white wall of the **Museo Naval** (Tue–Sat 10am–1.30pm and 4– 7.30pm, Sun 11am–2pm), which is not particularly interesting, especially if you are short of time. Follow the quayside, passing a row of restaurants on the left.

Pass the fishing port buildings and you will arrive at a car park. Walk under the triple arch to your left and you will be in Calle del Puerto. The second street on you left, Calle Mayor (Nagusia Kalea), leads directly to the **Iglesia de Santa María**, a church with a baroque portal. Facing the church, turn right towards Calle del 31 de Agosto, thus named because it was the only street to survive the fire of 31 August 1813. Ahead of you is the 16th-century Gothic **Iglesia de San Vicente** church. Bear to the left of the church

into a pedestrian square, Plaza de Zuloaga, where you will find the **Museo San Telmo** (Tue–Sat 10.30am–1.30pm and 4–7.30pm; Sun 10.30am–2pm). This Basque cultural history museum is in a building that was once a Dominican convent.

Cross the square in front of San Vicente church, bearing left, into Calle de Narrika (Narrika Kalea). Turn right down Calle de Iñigo to the arcades and café tables of **Plaza de la Constitución**. Returning to your stroll down Calle de Narrika, you will arrive at the busy Alameda del Boulevard. Turn right, pass a decorative bandstand, and head towards the waterfront. At the end you reach the Town Hall, a building which began life in 1887 as a casino. Look straight down the street to your left as you approach and in the distance you will see the city's neo-Gothic **Catedral Buen Pastor**.

Bear left around the Town Hall and cross the somewhat amorphous **Parque de Alderdi-Eder** and you will eventually arrive at the white railings above **La Concha** beach. This is the start of the **Paseo de La Concha**, which is, for the initial stretch, completely pedestrianised.

Above Left: the promenade, with the gigantic statue of Christ in the background
Above: celebrating a traditional wedding in front of the Iglesia de Santa María

Sculpture in the Rocks

If you have time to spare, it is well worth strolling along the beach to see the remarkable **El Peine de los Vientos** (The Wind Comb) sculptures, a series of bronze structures built into the rocks under Monte Igueldo by

Eduardo Chillida, who was born in San Sebastián in 1924. The wind resonates musically through the metallic creation, which has become as emblematic as any of the city's more traditional landmarks. You might also like to catch the funicular up to the popular funfair on top of Monte Igueldo. You don't have to cover the promenade by foot: the No 16 bus runs from the Alameda del Boulevard.

If you have the energy, follow the *paseo* along the beach for a number of other sights such as the **Palacio de Miramar**, built for the royal family in 1889 (the grounds are open to the public), and, further round, the Peine de los Vientos and Monte Igueldo. Of course if the weather is good, you might simply opt for some sunbathing on the beach.

6. THE HILLS OF GIPUZKOA *(see map, p32)*

This itinerary begins on the coast, passing the beach resorts west of San Sebastián, before turning inland to ascend the green valleys of the Gipuzkoa region in search of two contrasting shrines, to St Ignatius of Loyola and the Virgin of Arantzazu.

This route should be easy to follow, despite Euskera-only signs. From San Sebastián take the toll-motorway towards Bilbao and leave at exit 11, signposted to Zarautz and Getaria. (An A-road to the same point is less direct.)

Take the N634 through **Zarautz** (Zarauz), a former whaling port and now a holiday resort that counts as the Basque country's second biggest after San Sebastián. The road follows a terrace around the cliffs before arriving at **Getaria** (Guetaria), a town with several claims to significance. A brace of statues and a monument-cum-vantage point honour the birthplace of Juan Sebastián Elcano (or Elkano), the first man to circumnavigate the globe. This achievement is usually credited to Magellan but in reality he was killed in the course of the voyage. It was left to Elcano – who Magellan had manacled and condemned to death for mutiny – to command the expedition's only surviving ship, the *Victoria*, which sailed into Seville on 8 September 1522. Only 19 of the 200 sailors who had set out three years beforehand returned. Getaria is also the birthplace of the couturier Cristóbal Balenciaga (1895–1972) and the production centre of Basque *txacoli* (a tart white wine).

Getaria is undeniably pretty. Park somewhere just off the main road and

Above: a day in the sun for locals at Paseo de la Concha

basque country

stroll down into the town's steep, cobbled streets, which are punctuated by steps, tunnels and arches – all leading towards the harbour. Just before the harbour is a Gothic church with a floor that slopes uphill towards the altar, but so dramatically that supplicants could be forgiven for feeling that they are aboard a sinking ship. At the far end of the town you will find the Monte San Antón (also known as 'El Ratón'), which was an island look-out post until the 16th century, when it was joined to the mainland.

Continue along the coast to **Zumaia**, birthplace of the artist Ignacio Zuloaga (1870–1945). **The Museo Zuloaga** (Apr–mid-Sep: Wed–Sun 4–8pm) features the painter's works, and also some notable pieces by Goya, El Greco and Rodin. About 3km (2 miles) after Zumaia turn left by the cement factory on the GI631 for Zestoa and Azpeitia, driving straight through the once-fashionable spa town of **Zestoa** (Cestona). Skirt round **Azpeitia** (on your right). To visit the Basque country's railway museum, the **Tren Museoa** (Tue–Sat 10.30am–2pm, 4–7.30pm; Sun 10.30am–2pm), stop here and walk over the footbridge. Back in the car, continue under the green pipe of the iron foundry to the roundabout, at which you want to take the exit for Azkoitia, Zumarraga and Loiola.

The Most Famous Basque

Drive straight ahead at the traffic lights to another roundabout, where you should turn left, down an avenue of trees, towards the **Santuario de Loiola** (daily 10am–1pm and 3–7pm). This is a shrine to the memory of 'the most famous Basque ever', who was born Iñigo López de Oñaz y Loyola but is more commonly known as St Ignatius of Loyola (San Ignacio de Loyola, 1491–1556). Prior to

Above: Zarautz, the region's second resort
Right: returning to the pretty town of Getaria

his canonisation, he cut a colourful, dashing figure as a courtier, womaniser and soldier. Wounded by a French cannonball in defending Pamplona, he was twice given the last rites but survived three agonising operations, after which he was left with a permanent limp. Convalescence gave him plenty of opportunity for reflection. He changed his ways and moved to Paris where he applied his leadership qualities to founding the Society of Jesus (the Jesuit order) in 1534.

Built on the virtues of loyalty and strict discipline, the order became a force throughout Christendom, and beyond. Today there are said to be about 25,000 Jesuits throughout the world. The grandiose baroque shrine was built in the 17th and 18th centuries to a design by a disciple of Bernini, the greatest exponent of Italian baroque. The tower-house in which St Ignatius was born is almost lost in the middle of all this splendour. Restaurant Kiruri (tel: 943 81 56 08, www.kiruri.com) opposite the Santuario de Loiola does a reasonable, albeit expensive *menu del día*. It's a good idea to eat here because the further inland you drive, the less frequent restaurants become.

Continue on the main road past the shrine towards Azkoitia which, still on the GI631, you must circumvent to reach Zumarraga. Some way along the leafy valley between Azkoitia and Zumarraga you will pass the broken bridges of the old railway line. A short distance northeast of **Zumarraga** stands La Antigua, a 14th-century church which has some wonderfully decorated woodwork in its roof. Leave Zumarraga for Oñati (in the same direction as Bergara). After another leafy drive you come down to the stolidly

Basque town of **Oñati** (Oñate), most of whose population speak Euskera. From 1833 to 1839 Oñati served as the HQ of Don Carlos, Fernando VII's brother, whose unsuccessful claim to the Spanish crown ignited the Carlist Wars.

A Basque University

At the bottom of the town is the Universidad Sancti Spiritus, built in the 16th century by Rodrigo Mercado de Zuazola, bishop of Oñati and man of learning who wanted his fellow Basques to share the multifarious new forms of knowledge on which Renaissance Europe was at the time thriving. It functioned as the only university in Basque country from 1542 to 1901. You can still see the magnificent facade, which successfully blends pagan and Christian

Above: the Loiola shrine. **Left:** La Antigua's roof
Right: the Universidad Sancti Spiritus

imagery. A figure of Zuazola himself stands over the doorway. The facade, together with the cloister, comprise one of the finest Renaissance buildings in northern Spain.

Every year (in either May or June depending on the date of Easter), Oñati's most important fiesta, Corpus Christi, preserves a baroque flavour with masked and costumed characters playing the parts of Jesus, the 12 apostles and the archangel St Michael. While in Oñati you might want to sample some regional cuisine, in which case a good, reasonably priced restaurant option is Iturritxo (Atzeko Kalea 32, tel: 943 71 60 78).

Modern Shrine

From the ring road round Oñati ring take the GI3591 to Arantzazu, 9km (5½ miles) away. A shrine in a very different style to St Ignatius, **Arantzazu** stands in mountains above a gorge. In 1950 it was decided to build a new church here, allowing artists of the time free rein on a monumental scale. The result is controversial. The diamond pattern on the three stone towers was not inspired by egg trays as a cynic might suggest, but by the karstic rock formation of the surrounding limestone landscape. In the middle of the colossal carved altarpiece by Lucio Muñoz (which is far more impressive in reality than photographs) sits the statue of the Virgin of Arantzazu, who was found beside a cowbell and a branch of a hawthorn bush. Ask the caretaker and you might be allowed up the stairs behind the altarpiece for a closer look at the statue, which has been placed on a revolving drum.

From Arantzazu there is nowhere to go but back down the valley to Oñati. Retrace your steps along the road to Legazpi and Zumarraga. (If, however, you want to explore the Basque highlands in greater depth, **Bergara** and **Elorrio**, towards Bilbao, both feature handsome ancient quarters.) But to get back to your starting point by the most convenient route, follow the road through Zumarraga on to the GI632 for Beasain. Shortly before Beasain you are fed on to a motorway (still the GI632) and this road in turn feeds on to the motorway to San Sebastián. To the right you will probably notice the industrial town of **Tolosa**, which is best known for its red kidney beans (*alubias de Tolosa*), sweets and Basque berets.

7. NAVARRA *(see map, p44)*

A two-day trip to the province of Navarra, with a stopover in Pamplona.

The first part of the route can be awkward; if you get lost, head for the northbound N10 main road or A63 motorway towards the coast and the border with France and then rejoin the route at Irún.

Leave San Sebastián across the Puente de Santa Catalina (the most central of the bridges over the river) and take the main shopping street through Gros (Calle Miracruz, which goes on to become Avenida de Ategorrieta). The railway should be on your right.

After a while this busy thoroughfare brings you to the port area of Pasaia (Pasajes). This side of the waterfront is industrial but there is a view to the left of a pretty wharf. After crossing the railway turn off for Lezo and 'Portua' just before the tunnel. At a tricky roundabout take the exit for Pasaia-Donibane and Irún. Enter the town and bear left for Jezikbel (GI3440). Then ascend the hill leaving Lezo and after a short distance you will see a right turn on a bend again signposted to Jezikbel (GI3440). Now you can relax; the difficult part of the route is over.

The road quickly climbs to heights from which there a wonderful views over the sea. Only after the pass of Jezikbel, at 450 metres (1,500ft), does the route start to descend. Stop in the car park alongside the ruined arches for a tremendous view over the Spanish–French frontier. You can now choose between Spanish and French stations on the car radio. Come down the hill,

past the shrine of Guadalupe on the left, and straight into the fishing port and holiday resort of **Hondarribia** (Fuenterrabia), at the mouth of the Bidasoa estuary. The road wends its way around the 15th-century walls: park anywhere outside the walls and take a leisurely stroll through the old town, which centres on a castle (which now serves as a Parador hotel).

From Hondarribia continue on the road on which you arrived, towards Irún and 'Frantzia via Behobia'. This route takes you alongside the banks of the Río Bidasoa and into Behobia. On the left you will notice two white benches facing the no-man's-land islet of Isla de los Faisanes. It was on this little island that the Treaty of the Pyrenees was signed in 1659, thereby finally bringing the Thirty Years' War to its conclusion: this was the treaty that drew up the definitive border between France and Spain.

At the roundabout you have to choose between France and Spain. If you have another day to spare, there is a great detour to be made from here to the cog railway that ascends the mountain of La Rhune from a station situated between Ascain and Sare. You can then return to the route at Bera via Sare. But if your time is limited, turn towards Pamplona at this roundabout on the N121. The first town you come to, just off the road, is **Bera** (Vera de Bidasoa). Although Bera is quite picturesque, if you want to stretch your legs while taking in some local character, you would do better to stop off at **Lesaka**, 2km (just over a mile) off the road to the right.

The road to Pamplona follows the leafy Bidasoa valley, though a couple of tunnels smooth out the geography. In the middle of Oieregi there is an easily missed left turning (opposite the Hostal Urgain) onto a bridge which leads to the **Señorío de Bertiz**, a pleasant, well-organised garden (10am–2pm and 4–6 or 8pm in the summer) with a nature reserve behind it. After the garden, take the Pamplona road again over the Puerto le Velate.

Bull-running in Pamplona

For most of the year, **Pamplona** is a modest provincial city, but for two weeks in July it is transformed into either heaven or hell, depending on your point of view. The bull-running during the Sanfermines festival, made famous by Ernest Hemingway is – if you're not too concerned with animal rights – an undeniably spectacular event; but in recent years it has attracted a youth cult of heavy drinking, blaring noise and nights without sleep. If any of this seems like a disincentive, don't visit between 6 and 14 July.

At all other times of the year Pamplona has much to offer the visitor looking to fill a few hours. Get your bearings with a coffee in the Café Iruña on the central square, Plaza del Castillo. The two sights most worth seeing are the cathedral (Mon–Fri 10am–1.30pm and 4–7pm, Sat morning only), whose interior is more impressive than the exterior, and the Museo de Navarra

Above Left: balconies in Hondarribia. **Left:** view of the mountain of La Rhune
Right: Pamplona's Café Iruña on the central Plaza del Castillo square

(Tue–Sat 9.30am–2pm and 5–7pm; Sun 11am–2pm), which has Roman mosaics and Gothic and Romanesque art.

Pamplona is the natural place at which to break this itinerary for the night: it has a variety of hotels and the old part of town is brimming with lively bars and good-quality eateries. There are two centres: the old town, which features the best sights, and, across a band of green space (Ciudadela and Taconera park), the entertainment, hotel and residential districts of San Juan and Iturrama.

Wind Turbines

In the morning, leave Pamplona on the Avenida de Zaragoza, the N121, towards Zaragoza and Madrid. When you reach the 18th-century Noáin aqueduct – via which Pamplona used to receive its water supply – either take the main road for Tudela, Zaragoza and Madrid or take a short, cheap stretch of motorway. The horizons around here are marked by long lines of wind turbines – a new and renewable source of revenue for Navarra. Leave the motorway at the Tafalla/Olite exit and drive towards **Olite**.

All else is eclipsed here by the cluster of old buildings at the centre of town. The old castle, now a Parador, is next to the Iglesia de Santa María, whose carved portal depicts biblical scenes. But the main attraction is the **Palacio Real de Olite** (10am–2pm and 4–6pm; closes 7pm in Apr–Jun and Sep, 8pm in Jul and Aug), a historically dubious reconstruction of the castle of Navarra's kings. The towers and battlements are a delight to wander around. In its time the castle, built by Charles III in 1406, was said to constitute one of the most luxurious palaces in Europe, with its Gothic labyrinth of patios, staircases, galleries, towers and turrets.

From Olite return towards the motorway on which you arrived but continue into Tafalla and turn left on to the NA132 for Estella (Lizarra). The layout of **Estella** is at first confusing – park the car (there is a large car park next to the bus station) and try to navigate on foot. On the other side of the river you will find the tourist information office adjacent to the **Palacio de los Reyes de Navarra**. Up a flight of steps opposite

Above: playing on a modern addition to a reconstruction of the Palacio Real de Olite

is the church of **San Pedro de la Rúa** (guided tours only – ask in the tourist information office), which has a carved portal and a pretty cloister. Other fine Romanesque carvings adorn the portals of two other churches: **Santo Sepulcro**, on the same side of the river and the **San Miguel**, raised above the opposite bank.

There are surprisingly few good restaurants in Estella. If expense is no object try Navarra (Calle Gustavo de Maetzu 16, tel: 948 55 00 40). Alternatively, if you want a decent, good-value meal, Casanova (Calle Fray Wenceslao de Oñate 7; tel: 948 55 28 09) is a recommended option.

Puente la Reina

From Estella, head back towards Pamplona on the N111. You are following the road to Santiago de Compostela but in the opposite direction to pilgrim traffic. After 20km (12 miles) you reach one of the meeting points of the two main branches of the pilgrimage route, **Puente la Reina**.

You can see the old humpbacked bridge on your left as you enter town. If you didn't eat in Estella, you could try the Mesón del Peregrino (tel: 948 34 00 75) on the main road, a well-known, fairly expensive restaurant with accommodation.

Continue on the N111 to Pamplona over the Puerto del Perdón. There is no need to enter Pamplona. Turn off for San Sebastián and the airport. Follow the signs for San Sebastián and take either the N204 or pay a small toll for a faster drive along the first 16km (10 miles) of the A15. After that the A15 is free all the way to San Sebastián.

Above: resting at the Iglesia de Santa María
Right: pilgrim en route to Santiago de Compostela

Asturias &
Cantabria

The base for the following two itineraries is the Picos de Europa. This chain of limestone mountains rises from the Atlantic shore to heights of 2,600 metres (8,500ft) within 25km (15 miles). The Picos are bordered by the Río Sella to the west and by the Deva to the east. The Río Cares and its tributary, the Duje, divide the mountains into three great blocs or massifs: El Cornión (west), Los Urrieles (middle) and Andara (east). Each of the rivers carves a deep gorge, a *garganta* or *desfiladero*. The highest peak is the 2,650-metre (8,700-ft) Torre Cerredo; the most distinctive mountain is Pico Urriello, better known as Naranjo de Bulnes. In addition to rising high above the land, the Picos also descend into the depths: here you will find the fourth deepest cave in the world, the Torca del Cerro, which descends to 1,600 metres (5,225ft) below sea level. The roads on the next itinerary climb to 1,600 metres (5,250ft); the cable car to 1,850 metres (6,000ft).

The Picos straddle two regions of similar topography: narrow coastal plains where most of the sparse population reside, and mountainous interiors. In the west is Asturias (capital Oviedo), an ancient kingdom from which the Christians launched their Reconquest against the Moors; in the east is Cantabria (capital Santander). The southern part of the Picos strays into the province of León *(see Itinerary 9, page 57).*

Much of this mountainous area is protected under the aegis of the Picos de Europa National Park (for which there are information offices in Cangas de Onís and outside Potes). The whole region is excellent for walking and observing nature, with landscapes ranging from soaring crags to magnificent beech woods. There are 15 species of bat within the national park, 150 species of bird and 40 species of orchid among a rich flora. Most famous of all are the Pico's butterflies – 145 different kinds, some with irresistible names like silky ringlet, Queen of Spain fritillary and purple-shot copper.

Although activity tourism is now a prime source of the locals' livelihood within the Picos, traditional life still clings on. This is, for instance, one of the areas of Europe that produces the greatest number of traditional cheeses.

8. THE COASTS OF CANTABRIA AND ASTURIAS
(see map, p18–19)

Heading west from Bilbao, leave the Basque Country and cross the green provinces of Cantabria and Asturias, which are sandwiched between handsome mountains a short way inland and an attractive shoreline of low cliffs, small beaches and largely undeveloped resorts. This route could be driven in a day with a single lunchtime stop but it's far better to spend a night at Santillana del Mar or perhaps Comillas.

The main road between Bilbao and Oviedo is the A8 motorway. This route begins on the A8 then opts for the more meandering old main road, the N634 (E70).

Leave Bilbao on the Avenida de Sabino Arana (named after the founder of Basque nationalism), which feeds into the toll-free A8 motorway, cutting

through the southern suburbs of the city. Follow the signs for Santander. Along the *ría* (as a river mouth is known in these parts) to the right you can see vestiges of the industry on which Bilbao was built. The motorway winds behind the coast, whereupon it enters the province of Cantabria, and before long you have a view of the first stop, Castro Urdiales, ahead.

Take the exit for **Castro-Urdiales**, and drive into town until you reach the harbour in which bob brightly coloured fishing boats. Park here or drive up to the Gothic church, the Iglesia de Santa María de la Asunción. The ruined Templar castle next to it has been transformed into a lighthouse. Resume the motorway journey and continue towards Santander. You pass over the top of the resort of Laredo (where an old quarter is lost among the apartment blocks), after which you can see in the distance the fishing port of Santoña. Between you and Santoña is the most extensive area of marshland on the north coast, home to saltmarsh plants and resident and non-resident waterfowl. Spoonbills are the most interesting of the migrants that stop here in the autumn.

Santander
The motorway leads you into **Santander**: follow the signs for the port and park anywhere near the ferry terminus (where ferries from Britain arrive) if you want to explore the city centre. Don't bother if you want to keep stops to a minimum: Santander is pleasant but most of its historic buildings were destroyed in a fire in 1941. One tapas bar worth seeking out, a five- minute walk from the waterfront, is Bodega del Riojano on Calle Río de la Pila 5.

Left: home in the mountains. **Above:** Castro Urdiales lighthouse. **Right:** selling vegetables in Santander

Continue on the road along the waterfront, veering left uphill at the planetarium, with its distinctive brown dome. After a short way, turn right and park to visit the peninsula of La Magdalena, where there is a park, royal palace and zoo. Return to the road and turn right to continue in the direction in which you were heading. Descend into the handsome suburb-resort of El Sardinero, which is dominated by its gleaming white casino.

The Town of Three Lies

Leaving El Sardinero, cross the roundabout with a fountain towards the football stadium. Follow the road round the stadium that is signposted 'S20

Salida Ciudad' and Torrelavega. After a series of roundabouts you will find yourself on a dual carriageway. After crossing the Río Pas, take the exit for Santillana del Mar and Comillas. The signs direct you round an unsightly factory but before long you are heading through green fields to **Santillana del Mar**. This has been called the 'town of three lies' because it is neither holy (santa), nor on a plain (llana), nor on the sea (mar). To be fair, the first of the two 'lies' actually result from a misunderstanding. The name derives from Santa Juliana, a 3rd-century martyr whose relics are kept in the Romanesque church, La Colegiata, at the far end of town from the main road, where there is also a museum (summer: daily 10am–1.30pm, 4–7.30pm; winter: Tue–Sun 10am–1.30pm, 4–7.30pm).

Park near the crossroads marked by the Hotel Santillana and explore the charming cobbled streets by foot. These are lined with the stone mansions and towers of aristocrats and would-be aristocrats, most of them sporting coats of arms and pompous mottoes. 'Size isn't a dimension; it's a pretension,' the philosopher Ortega y Gasset wryly noted of Santillana's houses.

Santillana has any number of good hotels – many complete with decent restaurants – both inside and outside the historic section of the town. The Parador (tel: 942 81 80 00, or 915 16 66 66, www.parador.es) is the obvious place to stay if you can afford it, but there are numerous cheaper options: the Altamira (tel: 942 81 80 25, www.hotelaltamira.com) and Los Infantes (tel: 942 81 81 00) are but two examples. *(See Practical Information: Where to Stay, page 87 for further alternatives.)* It is a good idea to stay overnight in the town so that you can appreciate it at its best, early in the morning, before the coach parties full of tourists begin to arrive.

Santillana may look old but it is positively youthful in comparison with its close neighbour **Altamira**, some of whose famous prehistoric paintings may date back 20,000 years. To get to Altamira, take the Torrelavega road

Above: the traditional cobbled streets of Santillana del Mar

from the crossroads beside the Hotel Santillana and turn off right, following the signs. The caves are closed to the public, but the Museo de Altamira (www.museodealtamira.es; summer: Tue–Sat 9.30am–7.30pm; Sun 9.30am–3pm; in winter it closes at 5pm, 3pm Sun), opened in 2001, includes a replica, the Neocueva, which may satisfy your curiosity.

A Prehistoric Sistine Chapel

The main chamber of the caves has been described as a kind of prehistoric Sistine Chapel. Picasso said 'None of us is capable of painting like that'; Miró opined that 'Art has been in decline since Altamira.' Indeed, when the paintings were discovered in 1879 they were dismissed as forgeries on the grounds that primitive man was a savage incapable of such sensitivity and anatomical observation as seen in the pictures of bison, horses and deer. Working in a crouching position and, given the darkness, by artificial light, the artists exploited the relief of the cave walls to give naturalistic depth and movement.

Return to the crossroads by the Hotel Santillana and take the road to Comillas (straight on, had you not stopped to see Altamira and Santillana). Arriving at **Comillas** you glimpse the beach and this is indeed a good place for a swim. For more sightseeing, turn left and cross the town centre. At the end of town, turn left for **El Capricho** (tel: 942 72 03 65), a folly built by Gaudí but now an expensive restaurant. Comillas has other displaced Catalan Art Nouveau treasures such as the neoGothic Palacio Sobrellano by Domènech i Montaner and, in the cemetery, the figure of an angel by Josep Llimona.

Above: Gaudí's El Capricho
Right: relaxing in the sun

Carry straight on for San Vicente on the C6316, with the enormous Universidad Pontificia on the hill to your right as you leave Comillas. Turn right when you hit the main road, the N634, and descend to **San Vicente de la Barquera**, a fishing port dating back to Roman times, at the other end of a 28-arch causeway. Two sites make a stop and a stroll here worthwhile: the castle and, dating to the 13th century, the Iglesia de Santa María de los Angeles.

Unspoilt Port

The road climbs steeply out of San Vicente and passes near Unquera (known for its *corbatas* – sweet pastries) before crossing the provincial border into Asturias and approaching the coast's cliffs. Take a short detour to **Llanes**, a delightfully unspoilt port and resort with a few Art Nouveau buildings.

The main road now slips between the **Picos de Europa** and the coast: on a clear day you have good views left of the mountains. At Llovio, turn left towards Oviedo, following the Río Sella upstream. (A slight detour here will take you into the resort of Ribadesella and to the cave of Tito Bustillo, where there are prehistoric paintings.) In the summer months you will see hordes of people descending the river in kayaks, which can be hired in the next town, Arriondas. In August there is an international canoe race down the river. At **Arriondas**, turn off the main road for **Cangas de Onís**, your base for exploring the magnificent Picos de Europa mountain range.

9. THE PICOS DE EUROPA *(see map, p52)*

A round trip from Cangas de Onís, where stopover options include a Parador (tel: 985 84 94 02). Alternatively join the itinerary from any other point on the route – the town of Potes, for instance, makes a good base. This trip involves a number of walks and detours: if you have only two days you might decide to stick to the main route.

The roads of the Picos involve some steep ascents. They can be narrow, too, and exposed in places. Fill up with petrol as there are few opportunities en route. There are restaurants in towns and larger villages but, for greater convenience, bring picnic provisions. For the walks, wear suitable shoes and clothing, and carry food, water and a map. Check the weather forecast beforehand.

Take the main road out of Cangas de Onís, the first capital of the kingdom of Asturias, away from the town's principal monument, the Puente Romano (a bridge which, despite its name, is probably medieval rather than Roman). After 4km (2½ miles) you reach a roundabout. For a worthwhile 14-km (9-mile) detour, take the Covadonga turning here to visit the cave-shrine devoted to the Virgin, the patron saint of Asturias. In addition

Left: Puente Romano. **Above right:** local cheese
Right: mountain goats on the road to Lago Enol

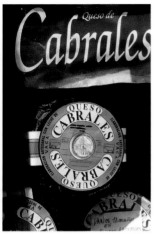

to the statue of the Virgin, look out for a statue of the legendary hero Don Pelayo, which commemorates Covadonga as the site of the first battle of the Reconquest in about 722.

The winding road continues past the shrine to two beautiful, high-altitude lakes, **Lago Enol** and **Lago de la Ercina**, but this would make a much longer detour – a round trip of about 24km (15 miles). From the roundabout outside Cangas, take the road for Arenas de Cabrales and Panes. This follows the valleys and northern foothills of the Picos, passing through towns well supplied with restaurants and accommodation options.

After Canales de Cabrales the road enters a gorge of the Río Casaño. You can get some good views of the peaks far above you as you approach Arenas de Cabrales, a centre for stocking up with food or souvenirs. One of the country's best blue cheeses, Cabrales, is manufactured in this area. From Arenas you can make a detour through the rocky gorge of the Rio Cares to Poncebos, the starting point of the Picos' most famous hiking route – along the rock ledges of the **Desfiladero del Río Cares**. This route has become so popular that serious walkers regard it as something of a pedestrian motorway.

Fiery Spirit

The main route continues from Arenas de Cabrales, through intermittent, often wooded stretches of gorge, to Panes, where you emerge into agricultural land. En route you pass the medium-price Casa Julián restaurant (Niserias, tel: 985 41 57 97). At Panes cross the river and turn right for Potes on the N621. You are soon back in a gorge, now the **Desfiladero de la Hermida**, which, punctuated by La Hermida village, marks the Picos' eastern edge. Near the top end of the gorge is the quaint Mozarabic church of **Santa María de Lebeña.** After this you emerge from the gorge into the pastures of the Valle de Liébana where *orujo*, a fiery local spirit, is produced.

The petrol station in Ojedo (before Potes) on the right is the last you will see for some time. **Potes** is the main town on this side of the Picos, and it

asturias & cantabria

is a good spot at which to stop for a meal, some shopping or an overnight break. A homely and inexpensive accommodation option is Casa Cayo (Calle Cántabra, tel: 942 730 150).

Relic of the True Cross

The detour from Potes to Fuente Dé adds 50km (30 miles) to the route but it is a highlight of any visit to the Picos de Europa. For this side trip, turn left towards the **Monasterio de Santo Toribio de Liébana**, which is 7km (4 miles) off the road. The monastery claims to possess the largest known fragment of the true cross, brought from the Holy Land in the 5th century by St Turibius, bishop of Astorga, and deposited here for safekeeping when the Moors invaded Spain. A scientific investigation ascertained that the relic does indeed derive from a species of cypress tree that is common in Palestine, and that the fragment could be 2,000 years old.

Slightly further along the main road, on the right, you will find a national park information office and, on the way to Fuente Dé, several good hotels. Two mid-price hotels are El Jisu (tel: 942 73 30 38) outside Camaleño and, at Cosgaya, El Oso (tel: 942 73 30 18), which also has a restaurant. The road ends abruptly at the enormous natural bowl of **Fuente Dé** with its ugly modern Parador (tel: 942 73 66 51). From here a cable car runs up to an 800 metre- (2,600ft-) high viewing platform. If you have four hours to spare, you can walk down from the top cable car station to Espinama (where there are a few restaurants) and back up the road to your car.

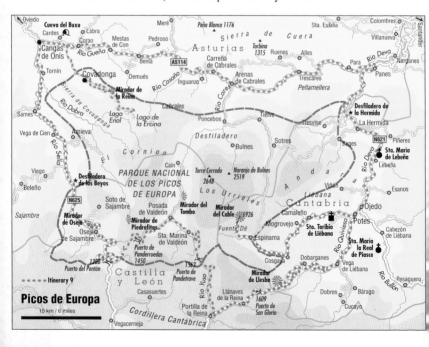

Picos de Europa

10 km / 6 miles

asturias & cantabria

Whether or not you make the detour to Fuente Dé, the route recommences in the middle of Potes where there is a junction indicating the continuation of the N621 towards the Puerto de San Glorio mountain pass. (Look out for a sign on the junction that tells you whether or not the pass is open.) Be warned that the road is relatively narrow, and rough in places. After a while it starts to climb, leaving the last of the villages in its wake.

Collado de Llesba

When you reach the **Puerto de San Glorio** (at a height of 1,600 metres (5,275ft), turn right on to the white track (easily passable by car, give or take the odd pothole) to the **Collado de Llesba**. Park at the turning circle and walk up the grassy slope to the white statue of a bear. There are some excellent mountain views from here. Back on the road, you enter the province of León and drop down through moors and high pastures to Llávanes de la Reina, where there is a single petrol pump if you need it. The road follows a mountain stream down a valley of wild slopes. Drive through **Portilla**, a one-horse town with a couple of restaurants before crossing a bridge. Take a turning just after the bridge for Santa Marina de Valdeón. This rough road leads to the **Puerto de Pandetrave**, from which there are fine views.

Entering Santa Marina de Valdeón, the road becomes a single track and runs along a pretty upland valley on a terrace cut above the river. You arrive at **Posada de Valdeón**, which is the de facto capital of León's part of the Picos de Europa. Here there are several bars and restaurants, including a highly informal, inexpensive eatery on the main square. Turn right at the square in Posada if you want to make a 3.5km (2-mile) detour to the **Mirador del Tombo**, from which you can look down the Cares gorge: this is the southern end of the classic Picos walk from Poncebos.

Take the road out of Posada (by this stage a proper two-lane black top), passing the Hotel Cumbres Valdeón and signposted to Panderruedas. Above the beech woods you will reach the 1,450 metre- (4,757ft-) high **Puerto de Panderruedas**. You might want to stop here to take advantage of the picnic area, and to walk to another outstanding viewing point. There's a pleasant descent through beech woods clothed in lichen to a junction with the N625. Turn right for Cangas de Onís, which is 46km (28 miles) away. After the 1,280 metre- (4,200ft-) high **Puerto del Pontón** the road leads down through woods (and a tunnel) to arrive in **Oseja de Sajambre**.

The journey back to Cangas drives through yet another gorge – the **Desfiladero de los Beyos**, which is narrower and greener, and usually less busy with traffic than the Hermida gorge. The road crosses and recrosses the river before entering the province of Asturias and eventually returning to Cangas de Onís, the starting point of this itinerary.

Above Left: the enormous natural bowl of Fuente Dé
Right: making hay while the sun shines

10. Oviedo and Leon   *(see map below)*

Drive from the old Asturian capital of Cangas de Onís to its successor, Oviedo, and on to León, following the history of local architecture, from pre-Romanesque to Renaissance, from one exquisite style to another.

This itinerary links two cities with few points of interest in between. It begins and ends in Cangas de Onís; but you could easily continue on to Santiago de Compostela from León via Astorga, Ponferrada and Lugo.

Leave Cangas de Onís across the bridge that runs parallel with the Puente Romano, in the direction of Arriondas and Oviedo. On reaching the outskirts of Arriondas you arrive at a roundabout, at which you should take the N634 for Oviedo. Approaching **Oviedo**, the road becomes a motorway. Follow the signs for 'Oviedo Centro' and the cathedral appears on a hill in front of you. On the right you pass the largest of the city's pre-Romanesque churches, **San Julián de los Prados**, which is decorated with frescoes. Treat it as an extra to this tour, however, rather than an essential stop. Drive straight ahead at the roundabout with a fountain for 'Centro Ciudad'.

You will soon arrive at a large, rectangular public park, the **Campo de San Francisco**. Park here (your best bet is a subterranean car park on your left immediately before the Campo) and walk up Calle San Francisco, opposite the tourist information office on the park corner, and you should find yourself in the Plaza Porlier, where there is a bronze statue of a traveller complete with suitcases. Off this square is another, Plaza Alfonso II El Casto (named after one of the most important kings in the history of Asturias). There is a bronze statue here of La Regenta, the central character in the book of the same name by Clarín, as the writer Leopoldo Alas (1852–1901) was known. The fictionalised Oviedo, called Vetusta, in which *Regenta* is set, epitomises staid, 19th-century Spanish provinciality.

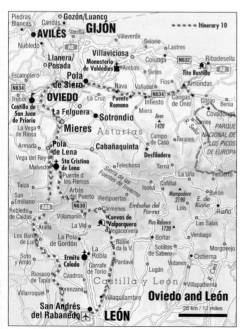

Medieval Marketing

The **cathedral** (Mon–Fri 10am–1pm, 4–7pm, Sat closes at 6pm) dominates this square. Although essentially Gothic, the cathedral incorporates a very ancient element, the Cámara Santa, a chapel which Alfonso II had built in the 9th century to hold a chest full of relics brought back from the Holy Land. In a calculated act of medieval marketing, he hoped he would convert Oviedo into a holy city attracting pilgrims in the same way that Toledo had done until it was taken by the Moors. In the 12th-century, decorative features were added to the Cámara Santa: a Romanesque remodelling that

asturias & cantabria

included the stylised statues of the apostles. Surprisingly though, what you see today is a reconstruction: the chapel was destroyed when fighting broke out between striking miners and government troops in 1934 and had to be rebuilt.

The two most outstanding buildings in Oviedo, both churches, are situated on a hill outside the city, and they are not well signposted from the centre. To reach them, start by following the traffic around the Campo de San Francisco. Drive towards A Coruña on Avenida de Galicia, across Plaza de América with its spouting fountain, and turn right at the traffic lights. Head down the periphery of a little park whose main landmark is an ochre-coloured villa. This street, División Azul, will bring you to a roundabout, by which stage you should see signposts to Santa María del Naranco or 'Monumento Prerománico'. After a second roundabout you wend your way up a hill, leaving the suburbs behind.

Visigothic Traditions

When the roads are not too busy you should be able to park virtually next to the two churches; if not, there is a car park some way down the hill. The two churches are both in the Asturian pre-Romanesque style, which flourished between the 8th and the 10th centuries. The kings of Asturias thought of themselves as upholding the tradition of the Visigoths (who occupied Spain when the Roman Empire declined) and the architecture they commissioned initially drew on both Roman and Visigothic influences. Later, Oriental decorative concepts were imported from Moorish Spain.

Santa María del Naranco (summer: Tue–Sat 9.30am–1.30pm, 3.30–7.30pm; Sun and Mon 9.30am–1.30pm; winter: Tue–Sat 10am–1pm, 3–5pm) is arguably Europe's most outstanding example of pre-Romanesque art. Built as a palace by King Ramiro I (842–850) and subsequently converted into a church, it has two storeys connected by an exterior staircase. At either end of the barrel-vaulted chamber that forms the upper floor there is a delightful loggia or arcaded gallery.

Above: San Miguel de Lillo
Right: Santa Cristina de Lena

A short way up the hill is **San Miguel de Lillo** (summer: Tue–Sat 9.30am–1.30pm, 3.30–7.30pm; Sun and Mon 9.30am–1.30pm; winter: 10am–1pm, 3–5pm) which, unfortunately, is only a remnant of the church that once stood here. Pay particular attention to the delicately carved door jambs, which depict a Roman consul watching the performances of acrobats and animal tamers.

Drive back down the hill into the city and navigate the two roundabouts

to bring you back on to División Azul, but this time travelling in the opposite direction. Keep going straight and look for signs for Mieres and the A66 to León. The motorway is free to begin with. After you pass Exit 92 to Pola de Lena, look to your left , where you will see another pre-Romanesque church **Santa Cristina de Lena** (Tue–Sun noon–1pm, 4–5pm). This small hermitage, 40km (25 miles) south of Oviedo, is known as the 'Church of the Corners' because of its many right-angles, and some of its design hints at the incoming Mozarabic style.

To visit this church, leave the motorway at the next exit, for Campomanes, double back and take the bridge over the motorway.

At the Campomanes exit you are forced to choose between remaining on the motorway and paying the toll or taking the main road, which climbs steeply to the 1,375 metre (4,520ft) high Puerto de Pajares. The views from here are quite dramatic as you cross over the great mountain range of the Cordillera Cantabrica – which separates the north coast from Castile – onto the *meseta* (plateau) of central Spain.

Seven Tunnels

The motorway takes a different route through the mountains. Rather than climbing the heights, it passes through seven tunnels, one of which is more

asturias & cantabria

than 4km (2½ miles) long. In between the tunnels you can stop beside the Embalse (lake) de los Barrios de Luna. The two routes are so different, you might want to take the main road on the way to León and the motorway back, especially if you are exhausted after all the sightseeing. One possible detour off the main road (adding 40km/25 miles to the route) is to the **Cuevas de Valporquero** (Mar–May and Oct–Dec:10am–5pm; Jun–Sep: 10am–2pm, 4pm–7pm), caves featuring some beautiful natural rock formations.

Either way, you will reach **León**, once the base of the Roman VII legion and the capital of the kingdom of Asturias-León from the 10th century until 1282, after which it was left behind as Castilian Spain moved first to Burgos then further south. Today a city with a population of 148,000, León is an agreeably active place, complete with a university, whose wide boulevards and well-spaced squares mitigate against oppressive crowds. The most convenient place to park, if you can't find anywhere else, is the underground car park beneath Plaza Santo Domingo.

If you walk up the Avenida de Ramón y Cajal from the Plaza Santo Domingo you come to what is arguably the most remarkable achievement of Romanesque art in the country – the **Colegiata Real de San Isidoro** (visit by guided tour Mon–Sat 10am–1.15pm and 4–6.30pm, Sun 10am–1.30pm; in July and Aug 9am–8pm, Sun 9am–2pm). The visit to this architectural wonder concludes in the Royal Pantheon, which is covered with frescoes. One arch features a series of paintings that depict rural medieval life month by month through the year. Another painting shows Christ on the cross smiling, triumphant over death.

León Cathedral

It is only a short walk from here to León's Gothic **cathedral** (winter: 8.30am–1.30pm, 4–7pm, summer till 8pm). The cathedral is most famous for its 700 stained-glass panels, and the windows' colours do indeed dominate the interior. Deep blues, ruby reds, vibrant greens and luscious purples and yellows give the space immense richness and light. But it is also worth seeing for the carvings over the west front doorway (one depicts the Last Judgement), and a cloister that dates from the 13th–14th century.

Take Calle Ancha back to the Plaza Santo Domingo. León's third important building is straight down the Gran Vía de San Marcos, beside the Río Bernesga. The **Hostal de San Marcos** (tel: 987 23 73 00) was built in 1173 for the Knights of Santiago as a monastery and hospital but is now a Parador. The 300 metre-(3330ft-) long facade is a triumph of Spanish Renaissance architecture.

From León, there are several routes back to the start. The simplest option is to return to Cangas de Onís via Oviedo (taking the main road or motorway). Alternatively work your way across country to Riaño (northeast of León) and join the end of the Picos de Europa route at the Puerto del Pontón.

Above Left: the Puerto de Pajares. **Left:** the Real Colegiata de San Isidoro
Above: the Hostal de San Marcos facade, a triumph of Renaissance architecture

Galicia

I f northwest Spain tends to be green and wet, Galicia, the region in the corner north of Portugal, is the greenest and wettest part. As a result of its geography – an interior landscape into which are carved a myriad of smallholdings, and a coast of deep *rías* (inlets) – and its Celtic roots (seen, for instance, in its bagpipe music) it has been called 'the Ireland of Spain'. Galician culture is currently enjoying something of a resurgence, as seen in the increasingly widespread use of the Galician language *(gallego)*, but it would be wrong to infer that the region is nationalistic in the way that the Basque country is: it has no serious separatist movement.

The majority of visitors come to see one Galician city, Santiago de Compostela. And they have been coming for a long time. When the tomb of St James (Santiago), Christ's apostle, was discovered in the 9th century (an event now firmly debunked by historians as a political manoeuvre by the Church), a new pilgrimage destination began to rival the other main centres of Christendom, Rome and Jerusalem. Of the network of signposted routes, the Camino de Santiago (Way of St James), that converge on the city, the principal ones come through France, merging in Navarra and continuing as one across northern Castile and into Galicia. Every year, thousands of Christians walk all or part of the way from the Pyrenees; a large number of the people on the streets of Santiago are latter-day pilgrims.

Many Tourists, Little Commercialism

A place imbued with history and religiosity, Santiago is a handsome city, with a perfectly preserved pedestrianised centre of monumental buildings. It became a Renaissance university centre in 1501, and Galicia's administrative capital in 1981. Although undeniably touristy, its religious importance, and perhaps the character of the Galician people, have served to preserve it from the excesses of coarse commercialism.

Much like Ireland, Galicia is known for both its slow pace of life and its hospitality. You might be hard pressed to discover enough attractions in the city alone to keep you occupied for a weekend but the two itineraries that follow – city and coast – should be more than enough to justify anything up to a week's visit to Galicia.

There are small rural hotels aplenty and you can eat and drink well. Given the length of its coastline, Galicia has Spain's most important fishing industry. You will be served superb seafood which you can wash down by the highly-regarded white wines of the region's five *denominaciones de origen*.

Left: bagpipes are a staple of Galician music

11. SANTIAGO DE COMPOSTELA *(see map, p60)*

An easy morning or afternoon stroll around the ancient city. The route begins where pilgrims following the Way of St James traditionally enter the city but describes a slightly circuitous route to their destination – the cathedral – to take in the harmonious, pedestrianised complex of venerable stone buildings that makes up the heart of Santiago.

The compact historical city centre is easily explored on foot. This route is short, and with a map from the tourist information office you can shorten it further. The best way to take Santiago is at a leisurely place, with frequent stops at the many bars, restaurants and cafés. But keep some time and energy in reserve to appreciate the monumental cathedral at the end of the itinerary.

Start at the **Porta do Camiño**, a five-way crossroads near which stand the **Museo do Pobo Galego** folk museum (Mon–Sat 10am–1pm, 4–8pm; Sun 11am–2pm) and **Centro Galego de Arte Contemporánea** (Galician Con-

temporary Art Gallery, Tue–Sun 11am–8pm, www.cgac.org). If you have time on your hands you might want to visit either or both of these attractions.

Pilgrims arrive along the Rúa de San Pedro, which becomes the Rúa das Casas Reais after crossing the Porta do Camiño. Take this cobbled street up the hill. A few steps to the left, on Rúa Travesa, is the 17th-century pilgrim church, **Igrexa de Santa Maria do Camiño**. After a small square, the Praza de Salvador Parga, Casas Reais becomes Rúa das Animas. On your right is the **Igrexa das Animas** (All Souls' Church); a carving above the doorway depicts sinners burning in hell. A pair of handsome *pazos* (Galician mansions)

Above: one of many ornate Santiago doors
Left: 21st-century pilgrims

form a corner in front of the church.

At the top of Rúa das Animas, you enter Praza de Cervantes, on which stands an ancient church, the **Igrexa de San Bieito**. Turn right downhill onto Rúa da Acibechería.

Pilgrimage Museum

Take the first turning on the right, Ruela de Xerusalen (Jerusalem). At the end of this street you step into Rúa de San Miguel beside the **Igrexa de San Miguel**. Almost opposite, slightly further up the hill is the Casa Gótica, which houses the **Museo das Peregrinacions** (Pilgrimage Museum, Tue–Fri 10am–8pm, Sat 10.30am–1.30pm and 5–8pm, Sun 10.30am–1.30pm). The building is, as its name suggests, essentially Gothic, but it was remodelled in the 1950s; it's worth seeing even if you don't visit the museum. At the bottom of Rúa de San Miguel you are confronted by the facade of the great **Convento de San Martiño Pinario** monastery. The church, reached by a set of curving stone steps, is open to the public (Tue–Sun 10am–2pm, 4–6pm).

On leaving the monastery, turn right and follow the building along Moeda Vella alley to emerge in the **Praza da Inmaculada**. With your back to San Martiño, the pilgrims' doorway of the cathedral is to your right down a flight of steps. Stay on the upper terrace bearing left round the cathedral, following the arcade in a little wiggle past the Café Literario. You will arrive at the top of a broad flight of steps that forms one side of Praza Quintana. Go down these steps. The cathedral forms another side of the square, to the right.

The somewhat forbidding wall of the **Mosteiro San Paio de Anteatlares** is on the left. The building directly in front of you is the **Casa de Conga** (Casa

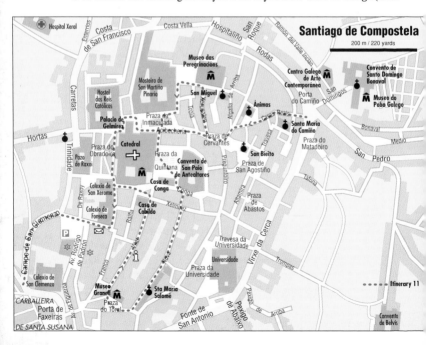

g a l i c i a

de los Canónigos), which has a broad chimney in the middle and an arcade at plaza level. Cross the square diagonally, passing to the left of the Casa de Conga, away from the cathedral. Take a dog-leg left and sharp right around the Café de Conga, crossing Rúa de Xelmirez to Rúa Nova – an attractive street of arcades. At the bottom, the Teatro Principal and the Igrexa de Santa María Salomé are to your left.

At the end of Rúa Nova turn right into Praza do Toural. Cross in front of the Pazo de Bendaña (topped by Atlas), which is now the **Museo Granell** (Mon, Wed–Sat 11am–9pm, Sun 11am–2pm) and turn right again into Rúa da Vilar, another arcaded street with several souvenir shops and a brace of tourist information offices (the one for Galicia as a whole is at No 43 and the one representing Santiago de Compostela is at No 63).

Biblical Characters

The end of this street is formed by the **Praza das Praterias**, onto which opens a Romanesque doorway of the cathedral carved with depictions of assorted

biblical characters, including Adam and Eve and King David seen playing the harp. Turn left at this square along Rúa de Fonseca, which follows the wall of the cathedral to reach the incomparable **Praza do Obradoiro**, a huge square that takes some time to savour.

The square is framed by four great buildings: the **Colexio de San Xerome** is to your immediate left as you step into the square. To your far left is the city hall, the classical **Pazo de Raxoi**, and in front of you the **Hostal dos Reis Católicos**. 'Hostal' implies a cheap lodging place and this one was built by King Fernando and Queen Isabel as a hospital for ailing pilgrims. Now the flagship of the Parador chain, it is anything but cheap. Look out for the Plateresque stonework adorning its facade.

The fourth side of the square is formed by the baroque west facade of the massive **cathedral**. Up a double staircase and through the main door you come to the Pórtico da Gloria, a 12th-century doorway carved with statues of prophets and apostles by an artist known as Master Mateo. It is traditional for arriving pilgrims to touch the central pillar to give thanks for their safe arrival – a depression has been visibly worn into the stone by countless hands. The crypt under the altar is said to contain the relics of St James. One fixture of the cathedral that is not always on display is the *botafumeiro*, a giant censer (incense burner) which is brought out and suspended from the ceiling to be swung during important services.

The cathedral museum (Oct–May: Mon–Sat 10am–1.30pm, 4–6.30pm; Sun 10am–1.30pm; Jun–Sep: Mon–Sat 10am–2pm, 4–8pm; Sun 10am–2pm) is in three parts, all entered on the same ticket. The crypt (in which there

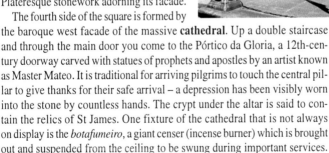

Left: market day in Galicia. **Right:** Hostal dos Reis Católicos

are carved capitals and fragments of stone crosses) has its entrance on the square while the door to the treasury and reliquary is inside the cathedral. The main part of the museum is entered from the right of the main entrance to the cathedral. Its four floors include the cloister, a tapestry museum and various rooms full of icons and statuary.

If, after seeing the cathedral, you can't face much more walking, turn right as you leave the main door into the Obradoiro square and down the double steps. An arch on the north side of the building lets you into the

Praza de Inmaculada. Go up the Rúa de Acibechería ahead of you and you will come to the Praza de Cervantes from which you can retrace your steps to the Porta do Camiño starting point.

A more interesting way to finish the day is with a view of the city. For this, turn left as you leave the cathedral and walk behind the Colexio de San Xerome and the adjoining Colexio de Fonseca to pick up the Travesia de Fonseca, which will lead you into the Rúa de San Clemente and out of the old streets towards a junction. Cross the road and you are in the **Carballeira de Santa Susana**, a park from which you have a fine view of the cathedral and the maze of monumental streets from which you have just emerged.

12. Rias Baixas *(see map, p64)*

The most attractive part of Galicia's indented Atlantic coastline is the Rías Baixas. This itinerary tackles only some of its numerous *rías* (estuaries) but covers enough natural attractions for two or three days. There are nice small hotels, and lots of seafood and local white wines.

The Galicia scenery is sometimes shrouded by fog and rain, but if the weather looks good, take swimming gear and allow time to enjoy some great beaches.

Leave Santiago either on the A-9 toll motorway or the N550 main road towards Pontevedra. If you are on the motorway, take exit 93 for **Padrón**. In the church of this little town is what is said to be the mooring stone used to tether the boat which brought the remains of St James (Santiago) to Spain. Just outside town, in a pretty garden next to the railway line, is the house-cum-museum (Tue–Sat 10am–1.30pm, 4–7pm, summer till 8pm; Sun 10am–1.30pm) of Galicia's favourite poet, Rosalía de Castro (1837–1885). Padrón is also famous as the birthplace of the Nobel prize-winning novelist, Camilo José Cela (1916–2002).

Leave Padrón on the N550 towards Pontevedra. After crossing the river turn off the main road on to the C550 to Vilagarcía de Arousa. (Be careful not to take the earlier C550 turning towards Rianxo and Ribeira). Near **Catoira** you will see the first vines of the Rías Baixas wine region and, to the right, the stumps of seven old towers, the Torres do Oeste, which consti-

Above: Santiago's monumental cathedral

galicia

tute the backdrop to a renactment of a Viking landing in the first week of August. Keep straight on for the town of **Vilagarcía de Arousa**, on the approach to which is a wooded island just off the shore. Follow the signs to Cambados and O Grove which take you through a messy port area (keep following the shoreline). Vilagarcía straggles along the main road to the extent that it seems to blend in with the next town, **Vilanova de Arousa**.

From a roundabout just beyond Vilanova, take the road towards **Illa de Arousa**, straight on at another roundabout and across a curving 2-km (mile-long) bridge. This takes you low over the sea to the Illa de Arousa, an island covered with eucalyptus trees and pines. Arriving on the island, a left turn takes you on a detour to the **Parque Natural de Carreirón**, a wetland peninsula nature reserve. For the main route, continue on to the settlement. Bear left in the town centre, follow the road around the harbour and turn right at the sign for **Mirador do Forno**. This should bring you to a giant statue of Jesus Christ from which you have a magnificent view of the island, the bay and much of the coast. Retrace your route across the island, cross the bridge, and head to the second roundabout (on the C550). Turn right here to join the road in the direction you were previously going, to Cambados.

Wine Country

You will soon drive straight into the main attraction of Cambados, the handsome Praza de Fefiñans, a square forming part of a 17th-century aristocratic house *(pazo)* which is now lamentably used as a car park. The other sight you will be directed towards by the tourist information office is a ruined church-cum-cemetery, Santa Mariña Dozo, but this looks more interesting in photos than in reality. Cambados is a centre for the production of Rías Baixas wine and from here you can explore several *bodegas* (wineries – ask at the tourist information office). Cambados makes a good lunch stop.

Above: Illa de Arousa
Right: Praza de Fefiñans

Local hotels include a Parador (Paseo da Calzada, tel: 986 54 22 50).

From Cambados stay on the C550, passing vineyards and *bodegas*, through Dena and Vilalonga for O Grove. Beyond Vilalonga you cross the isthmus of **A Lanzada**, beside an attractive area of wetland. On the left here is one of the best beaches of the Rías Baixas, looking across the sea to the Illa de Ons.

O Grove ahead of you was an island until the 17th century when it was transformed into a peninsula. A road into the centre of the former island leads to the vantage point of **A Siradella**, where there is a nature information centre – from which you can get an account of the local wildlife, and of O Grove's principal industry, fishing. On the peninsula's north coast is **Acquarium Galicia** (winter: Mon–Fri 10am–7pm, closes 8pm on Sat and Sun; summer: daily 10am–9pm; www.acquariumgalicia.com).

A Toxa Island

O Grove town does not have much to offer except seafood restaurants but you will need to skirt through it at least to cross the handsome low bridge leading to the island of **A Toxa** (La Toja). From the bridge you may well see people wading in the shallows at low tide as they endeavour to collect whatever shellfish they can find. A Toxa island is small but it has a handsome spa hotel (Gran Hotel de la Toja, tel: 986 73 00 25) and a casino. Beside the former is a chapel completely covered in shells. When you've had a look around, go back across the bridge to O Grove, bear left (without entering the town) and head back across the isthmus.

On the mainland you are compelled to negotiate two roundabouts. Take the C550 'por la costa' (round the coast) for Sanxenxo. The VRG41 is not recommended because, although it is a fast option, it can be very confusing. (If you inadvertently find youself on the VRG41, take the Sanxenxo exit). Drive through **Sanxenxo**, one of the main resorts of this coast, towards Pontevedra, always being sure to follow the coast. You might want to take advantage of a good vantage point just before **Raxo**.

Combarro is a picturesque place

Above: taking the weight off their feet
Right: the pretty town of Combarro

in which to take a leisurely stroll and perhaps to have lunch. As soon as you reach Combarro, turn right off the main road – immediately after the bend on the road beside Café Bar Raybel and Banco Pastor – and park when you reach the harbour. Alternatively you can park anywhere along the main road and walk down towards the sea shore. The whole village is a pleasing labyrinth beginning with vineyards and market gardens by the main road and ending with a cluster of flagged streets, narrow passages, steps, rocks, squares marked by stone crosses, arcades, balconies and the numerous *horreos* – Galician stone granaries – for which Combarro is best known. The Taberna de Alvariñas *(see Where to Eat, page 71)* has a lovely terrace for lunch.

The Prettiest Square

Continue along the main road to the final stop on this itinerary, the city of **Pontevedra**, which was a port until the 18th century when the channel became too silted up to be commercially useful. Since then it has expanded but mercifully the old town, a handsome complex of stone streets and squares, has been left more or less intact. Follow the signs for 'centro ciudad'. There is a subterranean car park under the Alameda (off Praza de España) which is a handy base. The prettiest square is the **Praza de la Leña**. Here, on Pasantería, stands the **Museo de Pontevedra** (Tue–Sat winter 10am–1.30pm, 4.30–8pm, Sun 11am–2pm; summer 10am–2.15pm, 5–8.45pm), which is housed in two 18th-century mansions and which has prehistoric collections, Celtic treasures and maritime exhibits. The town's most important church is the **Basílica Menor de Santa María**, built in the 16th century with a Plateresque facade.

From Pontevedra you might want to continue your explorations of this beautiful region. If so, head south through the rest of the Rías Baixas as far as Baiona. Or you could turn inland and head for León, via Ourense and Ponferrada, to join up with itinerary 10. The simplest option – and the only one if you have a flight to catch – is to take either the toll motorway or the main road north to Santiago de Compostela.

Leisure *Activities*

SHOPPING

There is probably not much you can buy in Spain that is not on sale in London and New York. Spain was once known as a cheap place to shop and as a country that produces an abundance of crafts, but a rising standard of living and a decline in traditional lifestyles have changed the picture somewhat.

Still, there are worthwhile souvenirs to be had. The most common craft objects in the north – deriving from the quantity of hard-wood forests – are of carved wood. Some pottery is produced in Galicia, Asturias and the Basque country, with lace coming from Galicia and textiles in Navarra. Along the Route of St James and also in Santiago de Compostela itself you will find innumerable items bearing the scallop-shell symbol of the pilgrimage. A Basque beret makes another original and evocative souvenir.

The clichéd souvenir from anywhere in Spain is the leather drinking bottle known as a *bota*. Filled with water or wine for a hike this can be surprisingly useful if you can master the art of drinking from one.

Shops are usually open Mon–Sat 9am–1 or 1.30pm and 4 or 5–8pm. Some shops close on Saturday afternoons. Very few shops are open on Sundays. Department stores and hypermarkets on the outskirts of big cities (look for signs to *centro comercial)* tend to have continuous opening hours, generally from 10am to 10pm.

Bilbao is by far the best city for all-round shopping. The stylish shops (interior designs and fashions) are in the Ensanche, off the Gran Vía. Older and more interesting shops are found in the Casco Viejo. Five minutes outside the city on the motorway towards Santander is Max Center, a complex of more than 150 shops and a hypermarket.

It can also be fascinating to browse in the everyday specialised shops that still cling on to tradition in modern Spain. Among these are *ferreterías* (ironmongers for hard-ware and tools), *droguerías* (for household goods) and the various food outlets *(see below)*. Other functional shops of which you should be aware are *farmacias* (chemists), *librerías* (bookshops, which are often combined with a stationers, *papelería*), *kioskos* (newsstands) and the all-purpose *estancos* (somewhat confusingly marked 'Tabac' outside); these state-licensed tobacconists also sell everyday items such as stamps, bus passes and phone cards.

A good one-stop place to shop wherever you are in the country is El Corte Inglés, a quality department store. There are branches in Bilbao, Burgos, León, Santander, Oviedo and Santiago de Compostela, each with a supermarket that sells imported foods, books, maps and a music department where you can get contemporary and traditional Spanish music on CD.

Food and Wine

Shopping for food in a foreign country can serve as a good way to get to know the local people and to understand something of the various native cultures. Even a standard supermarket can be exotic if you are at all curious as to what the locals eat. But for a better appreciation, go to the smaller shops: get your bread from a neighbourhood bakery *(panadería* or *horno)*; fruit and vegetables from a *frutería*; meat from a *carnicería*; sausages *(chorizos)* and cold meats from a *charcutería*; and virtually anything else from a grocer's *(ultramarinos, tienda de comestibles* or *tienda de alimentación)*.

In a covered market *(mercado)* – all of the larger towns have one – you will find

Left: looking for a souvenir
Right: cheese is a regional forte

stalls selling everything you need under the same roof. The weekly street markets *(mercadillos)* usually have food stalls, too, but they are best for cheap clothing and household goods. Both kinds of market are generally open in the morning only.

One forte of the north of Spain is cheese. Try the tangy blue Cabrales from the Picos de Europa, Idiazábal, a ewe's milk cheese made in the Basque country, or Galicia's *tetilla*, a soft cheese in the shape of a breast.

Although northern Spain doesn't produce the cured ham, *jamón serrano,* so typical of Spain, you can still buy it here. The best (and correspondingly expensive) is *jamón ibérico de bellota*, made from thoroughbred pigs fed on nothing but acorns and grass. No product from the slaughtered pig is wasted. After ham comes the spicy sausage *chorizo*, of which *chorizo pamplonica* – from Pamplona – is a renowned example.

Spanish supermarkets and food shops

have a lot of interesting items for sale in jars and cans. The seafood section will have a variety of *mejillones* (mussels), *berberechos* (cockles), *almejas* (clams), *pulpo* (octopus) and so forth – all of which can be eaten as tapas or used in recipes. Other delicacies to look out for include *bacalao* (salt cod) in the Basque country, and the canned and bottled pointed red peppers of Navarra *(pimientos del piquillo)*.

A number of places have their own, usually delicious, sweets which can make good souvenirs. Try Pamplona's *pastillas de café con leche* (a kind of toffee) and *tarta de Santiago*, an almond-flavoured pie from Santiago de Compostela.

Wine lovers will find plenty of choice in northwest Spain. Wine is available from supermarkets, from specialist wine shops *(vinotecas)* and – best of all – from the producers themselves. In most wine regions you can take your own bottles along to the local grower's cooperative and fill them up with good quality table wine.

Spain's premier wine region is La Rioja and the town of Haro has several *vinotecas*. Neighbouring Navarra, south of Pamplona, especially around Olite, also produces rosés by tradition but increasingly white and reds. The Basque country has its own small area of vineyards producing the sharp white wine known as *txakoli* on the hills around Getaria. Galicia is one of the success stories of Spanish wine making with the Rías Baixas region particularly up-and-coming.

Above: a neighbourhood grocery
Left: fine wine is sold here

EATING OUT

The Spanish tend to take their meals later than their European neighbours. Many Spaniards have a light breakfast on waking and a mini-meal halfway through the morning (at around 10.30 or 11am). Most restaurants don't open until 1.30pm and will expect to serve meals to about 3.30pm.

Dinner is always eaten late (9pm to 10.30pm is typical) but you can always have *merienda* – a light afternoon snack at a *pastelería* or café at about 6 or 7pm. Big cities have the usual fast-food chains which stay open from early until late without a break. And at any time of day there are *tapas* (also known as *pinchos/pintxos* and *banderillas*) at bars everywhere: if you want more than a morsel to go with a drink, order a *ración* (a full plate).

Places which serve food go by a variety of names other than *restaurante*. When it comes to inns, *mesón*, *posada* and *tasca* are all examples of traditional nomenclature. The speciality of an *asador* is roasting meat; a *marisquería* will have little else on the menu other than seafood. The simplest restaurants style themselves as a *casa de comidas*, a 'a house of food'. Almost every bar serves something to eat: sandwiches and *tapas* constitute the minimum: many bars have a dining room (*comedor*) attached.

The most economical option for a full meal is always the *menú del día*. Sometimes this will be a wholesome home-cooked meal but it is always pot luck, in more senses than one. The price may or not include dessert, drinks and VAT (IVA) – which otherwise will be added to your bill at seven percent.

At the cheaper end of the scale, many restaurants do not list their choices on a printed menu, and even if there is one, special dishes of the day may not be on it. Be ready for your breathless waiter to spout the list of choices aloud for you to choose. Don't be intimidated: ask him to repeat or explain anything you didn't catch.

Spain in general is a carnivorous nation and only in the largest cities will you find vegetarian restaurants. But even the tiniest place should rustle up something simple to order if you explain your preference, even if it is only a salad or *tortilla de patata*.

Right: dish of the day, with local wine

The Food of Northwest Spain
The Basques are the culinary masters of Spain and Gipuzkoa (around San Sebastián) claims to have the most Michelin stars per square kilometre. But if you are looking for a decent meal rather than a work of art you should eat well anywhere in northwest Spain.

All along the north coast good fish and seafood is landed by the boatload. Menus everywhere within reach of the sea (and often beyond) will have hake *(merluza)*, monkfish *(rape)*, white tuna fish *(atún)*, mussels *(mejillones)* and prawns *(gambas)*. Each region does its own variety of fish stew, which is always warming on a winter's day.

Meat-and-bean dishes are yet more filling: Asturias' *fabada* is by far the best. On the menus of Navarra, La Rioja and the Basque country you will also see *alubias* and *pochas*.

There is an excellent range of wines from which to take your pick. In Asturias and San Sebastián you will probably see cider being poured from a height to give it a sparkle in the glass. Rather than go for the standard international spirits you may like to try two local specialities: *Pacharán* from Navarra is made from sloes and served on the rocks; and *Orujo*, which is produced mainly in Galicia, but also in Asturias and Potes in Cantabria is often served as an after-dinner digestive – the variety flavoured with herbs is not as strong as the straight *orujo blanco*.

Restaurants
The following categories represent the typical price of a meal for one, tax included:
$ – budget (under 10 euros)
$$ – moderate (10–20 euros)
$$$ – expensive (over 20 euros)

Bilbao
Ein Prosit
Plaza del Ensanche 7
Tel: 944 24 13 11
A popular restaurant run by a Bilbao family of German descent. Try a hearty plate of homemade sausages and a Paulaner beer. $$

El Xukela
Calle El Perro 2
Tel: 944 15 97 72
A delightfully informal place at which to eat *tapas* or a light meal in the Casco Viejo. The surrounding streets are filled with bars and other small restaurants. $

Garibolo
Fernandez del Campo 7
Tel: 4223255
Popular vegetarian restaurant with friendly service. Open for weekday lunches and Friday and Saturday evenings. $$

Victor Montes
Plaza Nueva 8
Tel: 944 15 56 03
www.bilbaoweb.com/victormontes
An old-fashioned restaurant, bar and pavement cafe, with a mouth-watering display of tapas and an extensive wine cellar. $$$

Burgos
Meson del Cid
Plaza Santa Maria 8
Tel: 947 20 87 15
A hotel-restaurant in a large, 16th-century house (opposite the cathedral) which housed one of the first printing presses in Spain. Stout Castilian cuisine. $$

Estella
Navarra
Calle Gustavo de Maeztu 16
Tel: 948 55 00 40
Traditional Navarrese cuisine. Closed Sun night and Mon. $$

Haro
Terete
Calle Lucrecia Arana 17
Tel: 941 31 00 23
Haro's best-known restaurant, housed in an old bakery. Try the roast lamb (*cordero asado*) cooked in a wood-fired oven. $$$

Laguardia
Posada Mayor de Migueloa
Calle Mayor 20
Tel: 945 62 11 75
Restaurant (and hotel) in a 17th-century town house within the medieval walls. The best of la Riojan cuisine: spicy *morcilla* (blood sausage), *pimientos rellenos de bacalao* (peppers stuffed with salt cod), *chuletillas de cordero* (lamb chops). In a wine town, be ready for a hefty wine list. $$$

León
Mesón Leones del Racimo de Oro
Caño Badillo 2
Tel: 987 25 75 75
This former 16th-century stable serves game when in season, roasts and other hearty leonés specialities. Situated on the edge of León's lively Barrio Húmedo bar/restaurant district surrounding the Plaza San Martín. $$

Olite
Casa Zanito
Rúa Mayor 16
Tel: 948 74 00 02
Renovated old house in the town centre which is both a comfortable restaurant and a small hotel. $$$

Oviedo
Casa Fermín
Calle San Francisco 8
Tel: 985 21 64 52
This is one of Oviedo's most famous gourmet spots, and a favourite among local food lovers. Be sure to book a table in advance. $$$

Above: a *tapas* stop

eating out

Pamplona
Otano
Calle San Nicolás 5
Tel: 948 22 70 36
Typical Navarrese cuisine: game, trout, fresh vegetables. Good selection of desserts. $$

Erretegia
Estafeta 53
Tel: 948 22 56 13
A long *tapas* bar leads to a small, welcoming *asador* at the rear, where all the food used on the short menu is local, fresh, of the best quality and cooked in front of you. $$$

Europa
Espoz y Mina 11
Tel: 948 22 18 00
Somewhere to indulge yourself with rich Navarrese dishes immaculately served. Also an attractive hotel. $$$

Pontevedra
Doña Antonia
Soportales 4–1°
Tel: 986 84 72 74
Galician specialities including *tosta de vieiras* (shellfish on toast). $$$

Rianxo
Plaza de la Leña 6
Tel: 986 85 52 11
The upstairs dining room of this restaurant looks over Pontevedra's prettiest square. $$

Puente la Reina
Meson del Peregrino
Pamplona–Logroño road km 23
Tel: 948 34 00 75
Old and new decorative materials are tastefully combined in this restaurant–hotel. Traditional and creative dishes are served. $$$

Rías Baixas: Combarro
Taberna de Alvariñas (Casa Alvariñas)
Rua del Mar
Tel: 986 77 20 33
Inside, this restaurant slopes uphill with the rock it is built on, but you will probably want to be on the terrace outside, enjoying a sea view while you eat Galicia's trademark *vieiras* (scallops). Also offers a very good wine list. $$$

San Sebastián
Arzak
Alcalde José Elosegui 273
Tel: 943 27 84 65
Possibly the best restaurant in Spain. Book in advance. Closed Sun night, Mon and first two weeks of June and Nov, Jan–June also closes Tue. $$$

Beti Jai
Fermín Calbetón 22
Tel: 943 42 77 37
Seafood restaurant in the old town. Enjoy a full meal or *raciones* of anchovies or squid *(chipirones)*. Closed Mon and Tue. $$$

Casa Nicolasa
Aldamar 4-1°
Tel: 943 421 762
Traditional cuisine in a gourmet restaurant. The menu depends on what is in the market that day. Closed Sun and Mon night. $$$

Santander
Zacarias
Hernán Cortés
38 y Gral. Mola 41
Tel: 942 212 333
Cantabrian cooking, a good selection of local cheeses and a fine wine cellar. $$$

Santiago de Compostela
Casa Manolo
San Benito 3–5
Tel: 981 58 29 50
Enjoy a cheap meal in a renovated, cutting-edge interior near the sightseeing area. $

Don Gaiferos
Rua Nova 23
Tel: 981 58 38 94
Galician specialities (flounder stuffed with seafood, seafood brochette, hake in cider, and a light broth known as *caldo gallego*). Convenient central location. $$$

Vilas
Rosalía de Castro 88
Tel: 981 59 10 00
Galician cuisine, with specialities such as octopus with potatoes, lamprey in red wine, and the native *tarta de Santiago*, a moist almond cake. Closed Sun. $$$

NIGHTLIFE

The two rules of Spanish nightlife are: don't go out too early, and pace yourself. Spanish clubbers tend to carry on for hours. At weekends it is not uncommon to finish the night after dawn with a social breakfast.

Bilbao

The Casco Viejo (also known as the Siete Calles) is filled with bars. Other neighbourhoods that are good for a night on the tiles include Calle Licenciado Pozas, Calle Ledesma, Alameda de Mazarredo and the area of Indautxu. The neighbourhood around the Gran Vía tends to be for the staid. There are now several gay bars in the district around the Iglesia de la Merced.

For nightlife listings see the *Bilbao Guide* (published in three languages and available from the tourist information offices). Or check out the weekly listings magazine *La Ría del Ocio* for details of what's on.

Classical music, dance, opera
Teatro Arriaga
Plaza del Arriaga 1
tel 94 416 35 33
As well as theatre (in Spanish and Euskera) Bilbao's main theatre also has a programme of classical music, opera and dance.

Palacio Euskalduna
Avda Abandoibarra 4
Tel: 94 403 50 00
Classical music concerts and opera.

Cinema
Multicines
Calle Jose Maria Eskuza 13-15
Tel: 94 442 1876.
The majority of movies in cinemas (and on TV) are dubbed into Spanish. Multicines sometimes screens subtitled prints of English-language productions.

Live music
Cotton Club
Calle Gregorio de la Revilla 25 (entrance on Calle Simón Bolivar)
Tel: 94 410 49 51
Bar featuring performances by rock, blues and pop bands.

Above: Baie de la Concha comes alive
Left: pacing themselves for a long night

Bilborock
Muelle de la Merced 1
Tel: 944 15 13 06
A converted church near the river featuring local and other rock performers.

Astarloa
Calle Astarloa 5
Tel: 944 24 89 73
'Pub' with boleros provided by a pianist and a singer. Also karaoke.

Bilbaina Jazz Club
Sociedad Bilbaína, Calle Navarra
Tel: 944 23 14 03
www.bilbainajazzclub.org
Jazz and blues every Thursday night.

Discos
Distrito 9
Alameda Recalde 18
Tel: 944 23 00 56
Lively house music.

Crystal
Calle Buenos Aires 5
Glitzy transvestite shows.

Holiday
Avda Madariaga 18
Tel: 944 75 92 33
Upbeat disco music.

Oboe
Calle Ercilla 44
For the over 40s. Also live shows.

Casino
Gran Casino Nervión
Calle Navarra 1 (in the Sociedad Bilbaina)
Tel: 944 24 00 07
www.gran-casino-nervion.es

Oviedo
Bars in the old part of town, on Calle del Rosal, Calle Pérez de la Sala, and, on the cathedral's other side, Calle Martínez Vigil.

Pamplona
The best of the city's nightlife is concentrated in the San Juan and Iturrama districts, where there are numerous pubs, bars and restaurants.

San Sebastián
The best of the city's nightlife can be found in the Parte Vieja, around the Plaza de la Constitución, between the fishing port and the mouth of the river Urumea. The port features little taverns that sell fresh sardines.

Along La Concha there are music bars and discos, and around Amara Viejo FEVE station there are good *tapas* bars. Between February and May special *sidrerías* serve cider with steaks and *tortilla de bacalao* (salt cod omelette).

There is a casino on the Alamed. The city hosts a jazz festival in July and, in September, an international film festival.

Santander
Plaza Cañadio, the Paseo de Pereda and the streets between the waterfront and El Río de la Pila and Calle Carmen are well-stocked with *bodegas*, bars and restaurants. Or you might start the evening in Calle Perines or

Calle Vargas on the other side of the city centre. There is a casino at El Sardinero.

Santiago de Compostela
The prime streets for drinks and *tapas* are Rua do Franco and Rua da Raiña. Pubs and music bars are to be found behind Plaza de la Quintana in the San Paio de Antealtares district. There is a casino on A Toxa island near O Grove on the Rías Baixas.

Right: one of northern Spain's many options for gamblers

CALENDAR OF EVENTS

Spain enjoys a rich tradition of spectacular fiestas. At these events you should find a vantage point early and be ready to wait. Even if you are not predisposed to enjoy the occasion, you might as well see what is going on if only because sightseeing is well-nigh impossible at fiesta time.

January

In the post-Christmas period, Epiphany marks the arrival of the Three Kings on the night of 5–6 January. The occasion is a particular cause for celebration among Spanish children – this is when they are given their presents. In many towns the Three Kings participate in a procession, during the course of which they throw sweets into the crowd.

One of the first of the year's annual feast days is that of **St Sebastián**. For 24 hours, starting at midnight on 19–20 January, groups of uniformed drummers parade through the streets of **San Sebastián** in honour of the city's patron.

February, March

Late winter–early spring is carnival season, and the best-known Galician carnival takes place in **Laza**, in the province of Ourense. After midday Mass on Carnival Sunday the *peliqueiros* roam through the town wearing masks painted with fixed grins and Napoleonic mitres adorned with animal motifs. Be warned that the *peliqueiro* has licence to lash out at bystanders with the riding crop he carries by his side, without fear of retaliation.

April

Easter usually falls in the early part of April, and in the cities of old Castile, such as **Burgos** and **León**, you will find that age-old traditions still hold good. Here, for example, solemn processions feature the presence of hooded penitents carrying highly ornate *pasos* – colourful floats that depict biblical characters and scenes.

In a few places, however, the events of the Passion are remembered in a much more immediate, direct and painful fashion. In **San Vicente de la Sonsierra** in La Rioja the processions that take place on Maundy Thursday and Good Friday feature hooded *picaos* (penitents) who whip their backs until they run with blood.

In **San Vicente de la Barquera** (Cantabria), the period immediately after Easter is given over to a fascinating ritual when the local people set sail on a maritime procession known as La Folia.

A somewhat mysterious statue of the Virgin which, according to the local legend, is said to have arrived on a boat without any oars, sails or even a crew, is sailed across the harbour on a fishing vessel decked out in flowers and flags.

Above: decorating the streets for the local fiesta

May

Ending on 12 May, **Santo Domingo de la Calzada**, on the Road to Santiago, honours the miracles of its patron, St Dominic, with a series of processions. In the prettiest, the Procession of the Damsels, young women dressed in white with long lace veils carry decorated baskets of bread on their head.

June

Haro, the wine capital of La Rioja Alta, fights a Wine Battle on 29 June – St Peter's Day – in which thousands of people soak each other with red wine. It is squirted from *botas* (leather drinking bottles) but serious combatants use crop-spraying equipment. The tradition is to wear white, after which your clothes will always bear purple stains.

On the same day an unusual dance, La Kaxarranka, is performed in **Lequeitio** (on the Basque coast) on a wooden chest held on the shoulders of eight men.

Irún, on the French border, mobilises its men on the last day of the month for the mock military parades of the Alarde de

Armas de San Marcial, which recall the Basques' defeat of the French army in 1522.

July

The Los Sanfermines bull-running event in **Pamplona**, one of the most famous of all Spanish fiestas, begins on 6 July. Huge crowds assemble for the early morning *encierros* – both behind the barricades and in the streets along which the bulls will charge. Although the *encierro* takes only three to five minutes to run its course, it is a thrilling spectacle. The drunken, rowdy celebrations in Pamplona go on almost around the clock until 14 July.

St James' Day (25 July) is the biggest celebration in Santiago de Compostela. There are extra celebrations in a Year of St James, when the 25th falls on a Sunday.

August

The **Descent of the River Sella** (normally the first Saturday in August) is an international canoe race from **Arriondas** to **Ribadesella** in Asturias. You can follow the multicoloured mass of canoeists by car or on a train. After the race, the fiesta continues in Ribadesella, with singing, dancing and plenty of Asturian cider. Other canoeing competitions take place in the Pyrenees.

Both **San Sebastián** and **Bilbao** celebrate 'Great Weeks' (*Aste Nagusia* in Basque) around 15 August (Feast of the Assumption). The larger San Sebastián event includes an international fireworks competition – great firework displays light up the seafront every night.

September

The patroness of Asturias, Nuestra Señora de Covadonga, is feted at her chapel near **Cangas de Onís** in the Picos de Europa National Park on 8 September.

The various wine regions of northern Spain celebrate the grape harvest in August or September. One of the biggest celebrations is in **Logroño**, the capital of La Rioja.

November

1 November is **All Saints' Day**, on which the faithful take flowers to cemeteries to remember their dead. On 11 November, several towns in Galicia, such as **Santiago de Compostela**, celebrate Os Magostos, a fiesta in honour of the chestnut, hundreds of which are roasted on bonfires.

December

Christmas in Spain is a largely family affair rather than a public celebration.

Above: wearing white for Los Sanfermines in Pamplona

Practical Information

GETTING THERE

By Air

Bilbao's Sondika airport (tel: 944 869 663/4; www.aena.es) is the principal point of arrival for international flights to northwest Spain. There are regular flights to and from London, Paris, Frankfurt, Lisbon, Brussels, Milan and Geneva. Flights from the US arrive at Barcelona or Madrid, where a domestic connection to Bilbao is neccessary.

The cheapest option for flying from the UK to Bilbao is the low-cost airline, easy-Jet (www.easyjet.com) which has daily flights. Flying time from London to Bilbao is just short of two hours. Spain's national airline, Iberia (www.iberia.com; tel: 0870 609 0500 in UK or 902 400 500 in Spain) operates scheduled flights from London to Bilbao, as does British Airways (www.britishairways.com; tel: 0870 850 9850). Iberia also operates flights to Oviedo and Santiago de Compostela. Santander and San Sebastián can be reached by flying Iberia or British Airways to Barcelona or Madrid and taking a domestic flight.

From Bilbao Airport to the city

The A3247 Bizkaibus leaves Sondika airport every 40 minutes for the Plaza Moyna. The first bus departs at 6am and the last one at 10pm. The journey takes about 45 minutes, depending on traffic. A taxi is quicker but more expensive.

By Sea

P&O European Ferries (tel: 0870 520 2020, www.poferries.com) sails twice a week into Bilbao from Portsmouth. This route, aboard the *Pride of Bilbao*, is excellent for whale and dolphin watching and there are presentations and a guided wildlife watch on deck daily (for details see www.biscay-dolphin.org.uk). **Brittany Ferries** (tel: 0870 366 5333, www.brittany-ferries.com) operates a twice-weekly ferry service between Plymouth and Santander. Both crossings take over 24 hours. You will need to reserve a cabin and you should budget for meals on board when planning your trip.

By Road

It takes about 15 hours to travel non stop from Calais to Irún (just over the Spanish border) using French toll motorways. If you are taking your own car to Spain, headlight deflectors, two warning triangles, a set of spare light bulbs, a first-aid kit and a reflective jacket that must be worn in case of a roadside emergency are obligatory. Make sure you also have your driving licence and the car's registration documents. Your insurance company must supply you with a green card and a bail bond to prevent the police from locking you up in the event of an accident.

For information on coach travel to Spain see www.eurolines.com and www.eurolines.co.uk, or call 0870 514 3219.

By Rail

It is possible to get to northwest Spain from Britain via rail. For information and reservations, contact Rail Europe, 178 Piccadilly, London, W1, tel: 0870 584 8848, www.raileurope.co.uk, or see www.internationaltrainline.com.

Left: take the train from here
Right: the independent way to travel

TRAVEL ESSENTIALS

Visas and Passports

Visitors from EU countries require only a passport or a national identity card to enter Spain. US citizens, Australians and New Zealanders require a valid passport and are automatically authorised for a three-month stay, which can be renewed for a further three months relatively easily. Visitors from other countries should check with their nearest Spanish embassy before leaving home.

When to Go

There can be a great deal of variation in the weather in northern Spain, both regionally and seasonally. It may be sunny on the coast in mid-April but snowing on higher ground inland. Most importantly of all, this is 'green Spain', with a considerable amount of rain, so make sure you have a waterproof overcoat with you and practical footwear at any time of year. Galicia is particularly renowned for its mists and drizzle.

Although it is virtually never particularly cold in summer, you should bring at least one sweater for an unexpectedly chilly evening, a boat excursion or a visit to the mountains. In July and August, it is usually warm enough to swim in an outdoor pool or the sea. These are the prime holiday months when hotel prices go up and it can be difficult to find a room.

Winters can be cold and particularly wet around the north coast, but northwest Spain has a certain charm off-season. There will be less tourists around filling up the hotels and, moreover, this is the time to see visiting migratory birds. Spring (mid-Apr–mid-June) is a good time to visit, especially if you want to see wild flowers. In September you may also get good weather without the crowds.

As you cross the Cordillera Cantábrica to Burgos and León, on to the *meseta* (tableland) of central Spain, you will probably notice the change to a continental climate: hot summers and cold winters, and generally drier year-round.

You shouldn't plan to travel anywhere at the beginning or end of August, or at the beginning or end of any national holiday, particularly Easter Week, when the accident-rate on Spanish roads briefly multiplies.

Electricity

Spanish plugs have two round pins, and the electricity grid uses the 220 AC voltage system. Take an adaptor if you intend to carry any electrical appliances with you.

Time Differences

Spain is one hour ahead of Greenwich Mean Time (GMT) in winter, two hours in summer.

Children

Spaniards tend to be very fond of children and it is almost unheard of for them to be turned away from a bar, restaurant or hotel. Children go where adults go. Most people would rather take their children with them on a night out rather than leave them with babysitters. But there are not many facilities specifically for children: you are unlikely to be offered a child menu, high chair or nappy-changing room, though you can usually count on help from restaurant and hotel staff, and people all around you.

Disabled Travellers

Establishments suitable for the disabled are marked in the leaflets supplied by the Spanish Tourist Office. Confortel Hotels (tel: 902 42 42 42; www.confortelhoteles.com) is a chain of 11 hotels with good facilities for the disabled.

The local tourist offices can assist with details on facilities and services for the disabled in their locality. Visit www.tourspain.co.uk for good information and links for transport, access and assistance for disabled travellers. The Spanish Red Cross will also assist foreign travellers (tel: 91 533 4531;

Right: Spaniards take their children everywhere

www.cruzroja.es). In the UK, Holiday Care Service (tel: 08451249971, or +44 208 760 0072 from outside UK; www.holidaycare.org.uk) provide wide-ranging advice for disabled travellers. RADAR (The Royal Association for Disability and Rehabilitation) can also be of assistance (tel: 020 7250 3222; www.radar.org.uk).

Smoking

Although smoking is banned in a variety of specific public places – buses, metro trains and cinemas, for instance – it is generally permitted everywhere else.

GETTING ACQUAINTED

Geography

Spain is a country of 500,000 sq. km (nearly 200,000 sq. miles) and 41 million people. Northwest Spain comprises six regions – the Basque country (País Vasco), Galicia, Cantabria, Asturias, Navarre and La Rioja, and parts of a seventh, Castilla y León.

Government and Economy

Spain is a constitutional monarchy under King Juan Carlos I, who has been the sovereign since the death of the dictator Franco in 1975. The Parliament (or *Cortes*) in Madrid consists of a Senate and a Chamber of Deputies. The leader of the government is the prime minister.

The country is divided into 17 autonomous regions *(comunidades)*, each with its own legislature, though the degree of devolution accorded the *comunidades* is not consistent. The regions of the Basque country have the greatest autonomy (along with Catalonia), which includes the entitlement to impose taxes. The larger regions are divided into provinces.

Galicia has the largest fishing fleet in Europe, and the Basque country is one of the country's prime industrial areas, although the manufacturing sector has gone into decline. Farming is still vital to the economy of the northwest, although Spanish farmers often complain of the restrictions that result from EU policies. Rural poverty is still evident, particularly in Galicia. Tourism is also an important earner: most of Spain's 50 million annual visitors descend on the Mediterranean coasts but the northwest has become the specialist in back-to-nature rural *turismo*.

Religion

Spain is a predominantly Roman Catholic country with only small numbers of people belonging to other denominations and faiths. An understanding of, or at least familiarity with Christianity and Catholicism will help explain what you see in churches, cathedrals and monasteries, during fiestas, and in everyday life. In particular, many images of the Virgin Mary are venerated in Spain.

Above: the Basque beret symbolises a traditional way of life

Language

Spain's official language is Spanish (often referred to as *castellano* or Castilian), but it is not the only *lingua franca* you will hear in the north. The use of local languages has always been a contentious issue, but in the Basque country and Galicia there are two official languages: *euskera* (Basque) and *gallego* (Galician) respectively, though Spanish is also spoken. English is understood in most tourists resorts but a few words of Spanish and a phrase book go a long way.

Toilets

The country is somewhat bereft of public conveniences *(los servicios)*. The normal solution to being caught short is to enter one of the nearest bars – of which there is certainly no shortage– but you will normally have to order something to eat or drink as a pretext. If the doors have no symbols, men are *caballeros*, women *señoras*.

MONEY MATTERS

Currency

On 1 January 2002 Spain gave up its own currency, the peseta, to adopt the EU's euro currency. Some people, however, continue to think and talk in terms of pesetas.

The best exchange rates for travellers' cheques and foreign currency are obtained at banks. In tourist areas you can change money in *cajas de cambio* (currency-exchange shops). Carry ID when you exchange money. Personal cheques, even backed by a card, are not accepted anywhere.

Credit cards

With a credit or debit card you can make a withdrawal in the local currency from any suitably marked ATM machine (in cities and all larger towns) but your bank will probably charge a commission for the transaction.

Credit cards are widely accepted across northwest Spain, in restaurants, hotels, shops, petrol stations, museums and for buying travel tickets. Visa and MasterCard are common, AmEx is fairly widespread, but Diner's Club is rarely recognised. You may be asked for identification when paying by credit card. It is always a good idea to carry some cash, especially in rural areas.

For lost or stolen credit cards, call:
Visa – 900 991 124
MasterCard – 900 971 231
AmEx – 900 810 029.

Tipping

There are no rules about tipping in a bar or restaurant. After a few *tapas*, you might leave some loose change on the bar. After a full meal, it is usual to tip 5–10 percent of the bill.

Bilbao Metro

Plentzia
Sopelana
Urdulitz
Larrabasterra
Berango
Bidezabal
Algorta
Aiboa
Neguri
Gobela
Areeta
Lamiako
Leioa
Astrabudua
Erandio
Lutxana
San Inazio
Sarriko
Deusto
San Mamés
Indautxu
Moyua
Abando
Casco Viejo
Santutxu
Basarrate
Bolueta
Etxebarri
Ariz
Basauri
Kabiezes
Santurtzi
Peñota
Portugalete
Abatxolo
Sestao
Urbinaga
Bagatza
Barakaldo
Ansio
Gurutzeta
Cruces

Line 1
Line 2
under construction

Above: even banks have coats of arms
Right: the slow pace of street life

GETTING AROUND

Trains

Mainline, intercity trains are run by the state railway company **Renfe** (tel: 902 24 02 02; www.renfe.es; for international information, tel: 902 24 34 02). Two other companies operate narrow-gauge railways in northwest Spain. **Euskotren** (tel: 900 15 12 06; www.euskotren.es) runs narrow-gauge trains within the Basque country, such as Bilbao to Gernika and Bermeo and San Sebastián to Zarautz. **Feve** (914 53 38 00; www.feve.es) operates the useful north-coast route between Bilbao and Ferrol in Galicia. It also runs a luxury hotel on wheels, the Transcantábrico (www.transcantabrico.feve.es).

There are funicular railways in Bilbao and San Sebastián.

Main Railway Stations

Bilbao (mainline) Estación de Abando, Calle Hurtado de Amézaga, tel: 902 24 02 02
Bilbao (Feve services to Santander, Oviedo and Ferrol) Estación de Santander, Bailen 2, tel: 944 25 06 15
Bilbao (Euskotren services to Gernika and Bermeo) Estación de Atxuri, Atxuri 6–8, tel: 944 33 95 00
San Sebastián (mainline): Estación del Norte, Ctra. Francia, tel: 902 24 02 02
San Sebastián (local trains) Euskotren, Plaza Easo, tel: 943 01 35 00
Santiago de Compostela: Calle Hórreo 75, tel: 902 24 02 02
Oviedo: Uria s/n, tel: 985 24 02 02
Santander: Plaza de las Estaciones s/n, tel: 902 24 02 02
Pamplona: Plaza Estación s/n, tel: 902 24 02 02
Burgos: Plaza de la Estación s/n, tel: 902 24 02 02
León: Calle Astorga, tel: 902 24 02 02 (Renfe) and Avenida Padre Isla 48, tel: 987 27 12 10 (Feve)

Buses and Coaches

Buses covering inter-city routes are air-conditioned, with video entertainment to pass the time and sometimes onboard toilets. On longer journeys they stop at rest areas, giving passengers a chance to eat something and stretch their legs. There is no single national coach company: ask at the tourist information office or the local bus station for the company operating on your required route.

Main bus stations

Pamplona: Calle Conde Oliveto, 8, tel: 948 22 38 54
Bilbao: Calle Gurtubay, tel: 944 39 52 05
San Sebastián: Plaza Pío XII, tel: 902 10 12 10
Santander: Calle Navas de Tolosa, s/n, tel: 942 21 19 95
Oviedo: Plaza Primo de Rivera, 1, tel: 985 96 96 96
Santiago de Compostela: San Cayetano, s/n, tel: 981 54 24 16
León: Paseo Sáenz de Miera, tel: 987 21 10 00
Burgos Calle Miranda, tel: 947 28 88 55

Local Buses

Most local buses operate on a flat-rate-fare basis, regardless of how far you travel. You can usually buy a 10-trip Bonobús or Metrobús ticket from bus information offices

hiring a car, it is usually cheaper, and less hassle, to book in advance rather than trusting your luck on the spot. All of the major international car hire companies, as well as several local firms, have offices at Bilbao airport.

To rent a car in Spain you have to be 21 or older, with either an international licence or a valid licence from your own country. It is usually necessary to fill in a blank credit card slip as a deposit. Make sure your rental terms include unlimited mileage and check the insurance cover, including the level of excess.

Driving

The best roads are the toll motorways (*autopistas*). Toll-free main roads frequently run beside them as an alternative, but these are likely to be slowed down by trucks. Almost as good as *autopistas* are the toll-free dual-carriageways (*autovías*).

Main roads (prefixed N and marked red on maps) are usually good options with clear sign-posting. Other roads are variable although there is no way to tell from a map whether the surface will be pristine or pot-holed. The road numbering can be confusing – some roads change their names when they cross provincial borders. Thus the BI2604 becomes the A2604 when it enters Alava province and the BU550 when it crosses the border into Burgos.

The speed limits are 120kph (75mph) on motorways, 100kph (60mph) on all other roads and 60kph (35mph) in towns and cities. Speeding, drink-driving, and driving without wearing a seat belt are all punished by severe fines, which are payable on the spot. Children must sit in the back.

Double parking seems to be a national pastime but don't think that tickets are never given or that cars are never towed away. Most towns now have a system of pay and display parking (indicated by blue parking bays). In bigger cities it is simpler to seek out an underground car park.

Give a wide berth to drivers who overtake in dangerous places or jump red traffic light – practices that are unfortunately quite common in Spain. In the case of accident phone the police on 091. Every road injury has to be reported to the police.

and *estancos* at a discount rate. After boarding the bus, you should insert the ticket into a slotted machine that you will find behind the driver.

Bilbao Metro

The thoroughly modern Bilbao metro has only one line, but it interconnects with local train services run by Renfe, Euskotren and Feve to form a convenient light railway network on which you can travel from the Casco Viejo to the Ensanche, and to the beaches at Getxo. For further information, check out the website www.metrobilbao.net or tel: 944 25 40 00/25.

Taxis

Spanish taxis are a relatively inexpensive way of getting around. Taxis are available if they display a green *libre* ('free') sign on the windscreen or a little green light at night. A meter on the dashboard will indicate the fare. When you flag down a taxi, the meter starts off at a minimum fee, after which it automatically increases with every passing kilometre. If you ask the driver to wait, he can charge you by the hour.

A supplement may be added to the meter price for trips at night, trips beyond the city limits or for luggage.

Hiring a Car

Public transportation does not extend to the country's more remote spots, and many parts of northwest Spain are best explored by car, in which case a fly-drive option is very often the most satisfactory for holidays. When

Above: Bilbao's metro is a thoroughly modern affair

HOURS & HOLIDAYS

Business hours

Banks and post offices tend to open Mon–Fri 8.30 or 9am–2pm. Some open in the afternoon or on Saturday mornings.

Museums and tourist sites are generally open Tue–Sun. Their hours vary but it should be safe to assume that most such places are open 10am–1pm and 5–7pm.

Chapels and remote monuments often have no official opening times and entry can depend on getting the key from a neighbouring house. This is quite normal and you shouldn't be reluctant to ask around the village until you find the keyholder.

Churches are usually opened for Mass in the morning and the evening and close at midday, although the main churches and cathedrals of interest to tourists will have formal opening hours.

Public holidays

The following dates are public holidays in northwest Spain:

1 January New Year's Day
6 January Epiphany
Thur before Easter Maundy Thursday
Friday before Easter Good Friday
Monday after Easter Easter Monday
1 May Labour Day
15 August Assumption of the Virgin
12 October Día de la Hispanidad
(Spanish National Day)
1 November All Saints' Day
6 December Día de la Constitución
(Constitution Day)
8 December Feast of the Immaculate Conception
25 December Christmas

Each region *(comunidad autónoma)* of the country celebrates a number of other public holidays of its own and each village, town and city also has at least one annual fiesta. On these days, virtually all of the shops, banks and offices will be closed and museums and public transport facilities will revert to Sunday hours.

When a feast day falls on a Tuesday or Thursday, the preceding Monday or following Friday becomes incorporated into the holiday to facilitate a long weekend or *puente* (literally 'bridge').

ACCOMMODATION

Choosing a Hotel

Spanish hotels are divided into five categories and awarded stars accordingly. Unfortunately this classification system does not reflect price, quality or atmosphere. *Hostales* and *pensiones* are both cheaper, simpler forms of accommodation.

Paradors

The state-run Parador chain has nearly 90 hotels, many of which are located in restored monuments of historical importance, such as castles and palaces. Paradors are quite

uniform in their comforts but price ranges vary. Special deals can make them very affordable. Paradors are located at:
Cangas de Onís (Picos de Europa, Asturias), tel: 985 84 94 02
Cambados (Rías Baixas, Galicia), tel: 986 54 22 50
León (Gran Vía de San Marcos), tel: 987 23 73 00
Hondarribía (on the San Sebastián coast, near the French border), tel: 943 64 55 00.
Olite (Navarra), tel: 948 74 00 00
Pontevedra (Galicia), tel: 986 85 58 00
Fuente Dé (Picos de Europa, Cantabria) See route 9, tel: 942 73 66 51
Santillana del Mar (Cantabria) Plaza de Ramón Pelayo 8, tel: 942 81 80 00
Santiago de Compostela Plaza de Obradoiro 1, tel: 981 58 22 00
Santo Domingo de la Calzada Plaza del Santo, La Rioja, tel: 941 34 03 00
For central reservations, tel: 915 16 66 66; www.parador.es. UK: tel: 020 7616 0300; www.key tel.co.uk. US: 1-888 427 7246; www.eparadors.com or tel: 1-800 2231356; www.marketingahead.com

Right: sign of the state-run Parador chain, which includes nearly 90 hotels

Selected Hotels

The following is a selection of hotels throughout northwest Spain. Many of them are small, personal, homely and welcoming. At the other end of the scale – in terms of atmosphere, facilities and price categories – are the often grand historic hotels. The remainder represent the best accommodation on offer in a given town or city. Any tourist office will provide a list of other hotels in its catchment area in all price categories.

Hotel prices are usually quoted per room rather than per person, excluding breakfast, and prices should be clearly posted behind the reception desk. Remember that 7 percent VAT (IVA) will be added to your bill.

The following categories refer to the price of a double room in the high season, with tax included:
$ = under 60 euros
$$ = 60–120 euros
$$$ = over 120 euros

Bilbao
Iturrienea Ostatua
Santa Maria 14
Tel: 944 16 15 00
Situated in a central location, and occupying the first and second floors of an old house in the Casco Viejo, Iturrienea Ostatua is, by some distance, the most homely of Bilbao's hotels. The decorations are generally rustic though there are some modern touches. $

Carlton
Plaza Federico Moyúa 2
Tel: 944 16 22 00
www.aranzazu-hoteles.com
The city's top hotel. Orson Welles, Ernest Hemingway, Ava Gardner, and many great bullfighters have stayed here. The place breathes history. $$$

Bakio
Hostería del Señorío de Bizkaia
Calle José María Circarda 4
Tel: 946 19 47 25
www.hosteriasreales.com
A converted 19th-century building with 16 comfortable rooms. Close to the beach and near enough to Bilbao to make a base for visiting the city. Restaurant serves traditional and innovative Basque cuisine. $$

Burgos
Landa Palace
N1, km 235
Villagonzalo Pedernales
Tel: 947 25 77 77
www.landapalace.es
Delightful luxury hotel featuring a blend of old and new Gothic architecture. On the outskirts of the city on the road to Madrid. $$$

Cordón
La Puebla 6
Tel: 947 26 50 00
www.hotelcordon.com
A reasonable compromise between price and luxury, close to the city centre. $$

Above: echoes of the Moors' influence on the country

Cangas de Onís
Aultre Naray
Peruyes (north of Cangas de Onís)
Tel: 985 84 08 08
www.aultrenaray.com
A comfortable hotel (with only 10 bedrooms) situated near an old Asturian village and complete with lovely views of the Picos de Europa from its windows. To reach Peruyes, take a turning off the road along the Río Sella between Ribadesella and Arriondas. $$

Haro
Los Agustinos
Calle San Agustín 2
Tel: 941 31 13 08
A deconsecrated Augustinian monastery (in addition to being a former arsenal, hospital, school and prison) situated right in the centre of Haro, Los Agustinos comes complete with cloister. $$

Hospedería Señorío de Briñas
Travesía de la Calle Real 3, Briñas
Tel: 941 30 42 24
This delightful hotel, situated 3km (2 miles) north of Haro, is set in a large 18th-century house that served as the Italian headquarters in the civil war. The hotel is adorned with numerous antiques. $$

Hondarribia
Pampinot
Nagusia 3
Tel: 943 64 06 00
www.hotelpampinot.com
Cosy establishment situated in the old part of town. Before it was converted to a hotel, the building was a warehouse, cider brewery and aristocratic house. Maria Teresa stayed here before her marriage to Louis XIV. $$$

Laguardia
Castillo El Collado
Paseo El Collado 1
Tel: 941 12 12 00
www.euskalnet.net/hotelcollado
A fine castle-mansion with seven rooms and a suite, all exquisitely decorated. This is a good choice if you like a place with personality. $$$

León
La Posada del Marqués
Plaza Mayor 4
Carrizo de la Ribera
(23km/14 miles west of León)
Tel: 987 35 71 71
This is a comfortable and unusual hotel occupying an aristocratic house a short distance from León and well worth the trouble of seeking out. To get there, take the N120 from León towards Astorga and turn off right after 15km (9 miles) for Villanueva de Carrizo, cross the river into Carrizo and look out for signposts to La Posada and 'Monasterio'. $$

Oviedo
Hotel de la Reconquista
Calle Gil de Jaz 16
Tel: 985 24 11 00
www.hoteldelareconquista.com
Set in a spectacular 17th-century building, the Hotel de la Reconquista is universally considered to be Oviedo's finest hotel. However, it is situated quite a long way from the city centre. $$$

Pamplona
Maissonave
Nueva, 20
Tel: 948 22 26 00
This is a comfortable option located just off a square in the old streets of the city centre. Reasonable value. $$$

Ciudad de Pamplona
Calle Iturrama 21
Tel: 948 26 60 11
www.achotelciudaddepamplona.com
This is a good choice if you prefer to be based in the heart of Pamplona's entertainment district, Iturrama, rather than in the Old Town. $$$

Potes
El Jisu
Camaleño, Road from Potes to Fuente Dé
Tel: 942 73 30 38
This is a small, agreeable hotel, set in extensive grounds. Its location makes it a good springboard for walking tours in the mountains, and for sightseeing expeditions around the Picos. $$

El Oso
Cosgaya, on the Potes–Fuente Dé road
Tel: 942 73 30 18
A comfortable hotel that enjoys a tranquil location, and which is especially popular with foreign tourists. Approaching from Potes, you will find El Oso situated across a bridge from the main road at the entrance to the village. $$

Reinosa
Villa Rosa
Calle Heroes de la G.C. 4
Tel: 942 75 47 47
www.villarosa.com
As its name suggests, Villa Rosa is a pink villa, which can be reached from the bars and restaurants of the town, on foot, in 10–15 minutes. The bedrooms are cosy, and the friendly owner is happy to share his considerable knowledge about the area. $

Rías Baixas
Aldea Bordons
Bordons, near Sanxenxo
Tel: 986 72 43 74
Aldea Bordons is a tiny house situated in a hamlet not far out of Sanxenxo, but it is worth making the effort to find. It has been lovingly restored – with a mixture of old and modern materials – by the owner, whose family residence it once was. $$

Pazo O'Rial
El Rial
Vilagarcía de Arousa
Tel: 986 50 70 11
www.pazorial.com
Peacefully located within walking distance of the beach, Pazo O'Rial features its own swimming pool, and also a chapel in its ample grounds. $$

Pazo Carrasqueira
Carasqueira (southwest of Cambados)
Sisán-Ribadumia
Tel: 986 71 00 32
The rooms in this rural family house vary considerably in quality. The most charming aspect of Pazo Carrasqueira is the downstairs bar-restaurant where meals are served accompanied by the family's own *albariño* white wine. $$–$$$

San Sebastián
María Cristina
Calle Oquendo 1
Tel: 943 43 76 00
www.westin.com
One of the best hotels in Spain, the María Cristina was built in 1912 and still exudes glamour. Well located within easy walking distance of the sights. $$$

Niza
Calle Zubieta 56
Tel: 943 42 66 63
www.hotelniza.com
A small hotel on the promenade with a scenic view, Niza is perhaps the best mid-range choice in the city. Features Italian restaurant and a coffee-shop. $$

La Galería
Infanta Cristina 1–3
Tel: 943 31 75 59
www.hotellagaleria.com
Handsome French-style 1890s house with individually decorated rooms. Situated not far from Ondarreta beach and the Palacio de Miramar, and close to San Sebastián's shops and *tapas* bars. $$

Urgull
C/Esterlines 10-3°
Tel: 943 43 00 47
Centrally located *pensión* conveniently close to La Concha beach, the port and the old part of the city. $

Santander
Hotel Real
Perez Galdos, 28
Tel: 942 27 25 50
www.hotelreal.com
Dating back to the start of the 20th century, this elegant luxury hotel is situated close to Santander's main beaches. $$$

Las Brisas
Calle La Braña 14
Tel: 942 27 50 11
www.hotellasbrisas.net
Las Brisas is situated in a carefully restored old house, set back from the Sardinero beach and now unfortunately surrounded by modern apartment blocks. $$

Santiago de Compostela
Parador Los Reyes Católicos
Plaza de Obradoiro 1
Tel: 981 58 22 00
www.parador.es
This is one of Europe's historic hotels. It shares the square with the cathedral and has four arcaded patios with fountains, a museum, an art gallery and even its own church. $$$

Pazo Cibrán
Xan Xulián de Sales
(7km/4.5 miles from Santiago de Compostela)
Tel: 981 51 15 15
www.pazocibran.com
Ancestral summer house in a quiet location near Santiago (take the Ourense road and look out for the Xan Xulián turning after you cross the motorway). Immaculately kept by its Galiciaphile owner. Breakfast will fill you up for the rest of the day. $$

Casa Grande de Cornide
Cornide (Calo-Teo)
southwest of Santiago de Compostela
Tel: 981 80 57 41
www.casagrandedecornide.com
Stone house in a village 9km (5½ miles) from Santiago. Large garden with an 18th-century pigeon house. Some rooms have fireplaces. Take the Vigo road from Santiago

and turn left after 7km (4½ miles) for Luou. Turn right after you cross the motorway. $$

Santillana del Mar
Parador de Santillana del Mar
Plaza Ramón Pelayo 8
Tel: 942 81 80 00
www.parador.es
This is one of the finest buildings in this beautiful old town. Bare stone walls, pretty patio and tiled floors recreate a medieval atmosphere. $$$

Los Infantes
Avenida L'Dorat 1
Tel: 942 81 81 00
Hotel just outside the old town complete with original 18th-century facade. The rest of the building has been rebuilt, but is furnished in period style. $$

Altamira
Cantón 1
Tel: 942 81 80 25
www.hotelaltamira.com
Old mansion in the town centre. $$

Hostería de Quijas
Barrio Vinuesa, Quijas
(southwest of Santillana del Mar)
Tel: 942 82 08 33
www.hosteriadequijas.com
An 18th-century mansion off the Santander–Oviedo road (near Torrelavega) with a splendid garden. $$

Casas Rurales

If you want to stay in the countryside without the formality of a hotel, ask the local tourist office about *casas rurales*, basic lodgings in restored village houses and farmhouses. *Casa rural* can equally apply to a house rented as self-catering accommodation (minimum stay usually a weekend) or a guesthouse in which the owner provides bed and breakfast for a night or more.

Camping and Caravans

There are campsites throughout northwest Spain, especially along the coast. The website www.vayaspain.com has lots of useful information on camping in Spain. Or contact the Spanish Federation of Campsite Owners:

Above: at your service

Federación Española de Empresarios de Campings y C.V., San Bernardo 97–99, Edificio Colomina 3º, 28015 Madrid. Tel: 0034 91 448 1234. Fax: 0034 91 448 1267. Website: www.fedcamping.com.

HEALTH AND EMERGENCIES

Hygiene and Health

There are no serious health hazards in Spain and you don't need any special inoculations to enter the country. If you are an EU citizen, pick up an E111 form from any post office before travelling abroad. This entitles you to free basic health care within the Spanish social security system. You may also want to take out travel insurance which will include medical treatment as well as cover for theft and accident.

Even though this area of northern Spain is known for having more than its fair share of rainfall, you should beware of the sun. In summer, come prepared with a sun hat and protective suncreams. Try to keep your activities to early morning or late afternoon when the sun is at its least fierce. Drink lots of water, and take particular care with young children who have sensitive skin.

There are no particular food hazards to be aware of but you should avoid shellfish and anything made with eggs if there is no way to ascertain that they are fresh. Tap water can be drunk without reservations, but if you prefer, bottled water (still and sparkling) is available everywhere.

Chemists

Chemist shops, or *farmacias*, are identifiable by the big green cross displayed on the facade or hanging over the street. Pharmacies are open during normal shopping hours (Mon–Fri 9.30am–1.30pm, 5–8pm; Sat 9am–1.30pm). In most towns an effective rotation system ensures that there is always at least one chemist (*farmacia de guardia*) open around the clock. Pharmacists are trained paramedics and are authorised to advise on minor ailments.

Don't forget to bring any prescription medicines that you require. Although the country's pharmacies are amply stocked with medicines manufactured by international companies and, despite the ready availability of many common drugs – which can be purchased without prescription – you might have a problem finding your particular medication. Chemists in Spain do not honour prescriptions that were written abroad.

Confusingly, shops called *parafarmacías* are now appearing in Spain. They also display a green cross outside, but they sell beauty products, baby food and other non-medical products. They do not supply prescription drugs.

Security and crime

Spain is no more dangerous than any other western European country and most crime will be deterred by elementary precautions. Keep valuables in the hotel safe and don't carry large sums of money or your passport (take a photocopy instead), unless you are going to exchange money.

In crowds, on public transport and in touristy areas, be on your guard for pickpockets. It is a common strategy for a gang member to distract anyone who looks disorientated while another picks up your momentarily unattended bag. In the car always keep valuables hidden: there have been cases of opportunist thieves on motorbikes sticking their hand through open car windows. When you park your car, it is wise to leave nothing at all in view. If possible, always park your car in a garage or a guarded car park.

If you are robbed, remember that thieves usually want easily disposable cash and it is worth checking the nearest gutters, rubbish containers and toilets for your personal possessions: thieves swiftly dispose of unwanted items. If you are robbed report the offence to the local police. The police probably won't find your lost belongings but you will need to fill in a form for insurance purposes.

Emergency Numbers

Local Police (Policia Municipal/Local – for minor incidents) 092
National police (Policia Nacional, to report crimes in urban areas) 091
Guardia Civil (to report crimes in rural areas) 062
Emergencies, Ambulance and Fire brigade 112

COMMUNICATIONS

Post

You will only need to visit a post office to send special items – for instance you may want to send a letter *urgente* as the post to and from Spain can be painfully slow. Otherwise it is usually more convenient to buy stamps in an *estanco* (tobacconist), which can be recognised by a brown and gold *Tabaco* sign.

Telephone

The most convenient way to make phone calls in Spain (unless you are carrying a mobile) is with a phone card *(tarjeta telefónica)*. Those issued by Telefónica (available from *estancos*) work in all public phone booths (which also take coins).

A variety of other prepaid phone cards are also sold in *estancos* and other shops; these can be used anywhere by phoning a number and punching in a secret code. International prepaid calling cards are sold on ferries and planes. Use these cards in hotel rooms to avoid inflated surcharges.

Many bars have a green (coin) phone on the counter or a public phone on the wall – make your call then pay at the counter.

For directory enquiries, dial 11822 or 11818; for international directory enquiries, dial 11825 (they are both premium numbers).

Above: keeping in touch
Right: streetside newspaper vendor

To dial out of Spain, dial 00 followed by the relevant country code:

UK – 44
Ireland – 353
North America – 1.

The international code for Spain is 34. When calling a Spanish number, dial the full area code (beginning with 9) even if you are dialling across the street in a small village.

The normal way to answer a phone in Spain is to say '*dígame*' (literally, 'speak to me' or 'say something'): it's not rude, merely an invitation to the caller to explain what he or she wants. One useful piece of phone vocabulary is '*de parte de…*', which means 'on behalf of…', usually your own name.

Each of the larger cities in the region has one or more Internet cafés – ask for details in the tourist information office.

Newspapers

El País, *ABC*, *Ya*, *Diario 16* and *El Mundo* are Spain's national daily papers. Their local editions carry information on regional events as well as TV listings and duty-chemist details. Major newsstands in most major cities carry the *International Herald Tribune*, *Time*, *Newsweek* and the likes of *The Times*, *The Guardian* and the *Wall Street Journal*. Spain has some good English-language newspapers and magazines but none specific to the north coast. Among them are *Spain* and *Living Spain*.

Television and Radio

In addition to two nationwide television channels – TVE 1 and TVE 2 – each region has one or more local stations. The local Basque stations ETB 1 and ETB 2 have Basque-language programmes. There are

three private networks: Antena 3, Tele 5 and Canal Plus. Canal Plus is a private pay channel that broadcasts many undubbed English-language films – look out for 'V.O.' – '*Versión Original*' – in TV listings.

Better hotels have access to a variety of satellite channels, several of which – Super Channel, Sky Movies, Eurosport, BBC, CNN, Lifestyle etc – are broadcast in English.

The BBC World Service can be picked up with a short-wave radio.

BOOKS AND MAPS

Books on the main sights, some of them in English, are available locally. Each of the regional capitals has one or more specialised bookshops selling a good range of travel literature in Spanish. A good option for general books is El Corte Inglés, which has branches in the major cities.

The best series of maps for driving is Michelin's 1cm: 4km. Sheets 571, 572, 573 and 575 cover all the routes in this book.

For walking maps try Stanfords Ltd, 12–14 Long Acre, Covent Garden, London WC2E 9LP. Tel: 020 7836 1321. If you want more detailed specialist maps, contact Servicio de Publicaciones del Instituto Geográfico Nacional, which has a shop in Madrid, in Plaza San Juan de la Cruz. Tel: 91 597 61 87, www.mfom.es.

SPORTS AND ACTIVITIES

The Pilgrimage Routes

Northwest Spain is crossed by assorted routes of pilgrimage to the great cathedral at Santiago de Compostela. The main route, known as the *camino francés*, runs 800km (500 miles) from Roncesvalles on the Navarra/France border. It takes a fit person around five weeks to walk, or two weeks to cycle. There are pilgrims' hostels (*refugios*) along much of the route. Pilgrims carry a passport which they get stamped at at various points on the way.

For further information, contact The Cofraternity of Saint James, 27 Blackfriars Road, London SE1 8NY. Tel: 020 7928 9988, www.csj.org.uk.

Spectator sports

First Division football matches are a Sunday afternoon ritual across northern Spain – matches are usually played in Santiago de Compostela, La Coruña, Santander, Bilbao, San Sebastián, Logroño and Pamplona.

Pelota is the Basques' national game. It can be played with bare hands or with a wicker glove. Pelota is played on a *frontón*,

something like a squash court but open on one of its longest sides. The Basques are also passionate about strength sports derived from the chores or rural life: stone-lifting, log-chopping, scything, stone dragging (using teams of oxen) and tug-of-war.

Bullfighting

The ritualistic killing of bulls as sport appals animal-rights advocates but it is a longstanding tradition in Spain. Spaniards debate endlessly whether it is some kind of art or a sport but rarely whether it is morally acceptable. If you want to see a bullfight it is best to accompany someone who can explain the proceedings. Ticket prices vary according to the abilities of the *toreros* and where you sit – the shade is a good choice on a hot day.

'Bull-running'

Bull-running, either through streets or in a temporary ring during a town's fiesta, is something else. It is not usual for the animals to end up being killed, although Pamplona is an exception. At bull-running events, the animals are mostly brought out for the day and taken back to a farm in the evening; some of the animals learn to behave more intelligently than the humans baiting them.

Above: the symbol of pelota, the Basques' traditional game

USEFUL ADDRESSES

Tourist information offices

Tourist offices are usually open Mon–Sat 10am–1pm and 3 or 4pm–7pm. If there isn't a tourist office you might be able to get a map, leaflet or other relevant information from the town hall *(ayuntamiento)*.

The Spanish tourist office in London PO Box 4009, London, W1A 6NB, tel: 020 7486 8077 (Mon–Fri 9.15am–4.15pm), or 24 hour brochure request line 08459 400 180; www.tourspain.co.uk or www.spain.info

In Republic of Ireland, tel: 0818 220 290.

The Spanish tourist office in New York is at 666 Fifth Avenue, NY 10103, tel: 212-265 8822, fax: 212-265 8864, www.okspain.org

Tourist offices in Northern Spain:

Bilbao: Rodriguez Arias 3 (tel: 944 795 760), Plaza Arriga, and Abandoibarra Etorbidea 2 (outside the Guggenheim Museum), www.bilbao.net and www.euskadi.net

Burgos: Plaza Alonso Martinez 7, tel: 947 203 125, www.patroturisbur.es

León: Plaza de la Regla 3 (directly in front of cathedral), tel: 987 237 082.

Logroño (for La Rioja): Paseo del Espolón, tel: 941 291 260, www.larioja.org

Oviedo (also for the rest of Asturias): Plaza de Alfonso II El Casto 6 (in front of cathedral), tel: 985 213 385, www.princast.es

Pamplona (also applicable for the rest of Navarra): Calle Eslava 1 (on the corner of Plaza San Francisco), tel: 948 206 540, www.cfnavarra.es/turismonavarra and www.pamplona.net

San Sebastián Reina Regente, tel: 943 481 166, www.sansebastianturismo.com

Santander (also for the rest of Cantabria): Hernán Cortés 4, tel: 942 310 708 and Jardines de Pereda (opposite ferry terminal), tel: 942 224 995, www.cantabriaturismo.com

Santiago de Compostela Rúa do Vilar, 43, tel: 981 584 081, www.turgalicia.es (one of the better websites), www.santiagodecompostela.org and www.santiagoturismo.com

Rías Baixas tel: 986 842 690, www.riasbaixas.org

Embassies and consulates

The following have embassies in Madrid:
Australia: Plaza Descubridor Diego de Ordás, 3, tel: 914 419 300.
Canada: Núñez de Balboa, 35, tel: 914 314 300.

Ireland: Paseo de la Castellana, 3, tel: 915 763 500.
UK: Fernando el Santo, 16, tel: 913 190 200, www.ukinspain.com
US: Calle Serrano, 75, tel: 915 774 000.

If you don't want to travel that far for a consular matter, there is a British consulates in northwest Spain in Bilbao:
Bilbao (Consulate-General), Alameda de Urquijo 2–8, tel: 944 157 600/711.

FURTHER READING

Insight Guide: Northern Spain (APA, updated 2003). This ideal companion to the region includes evocative photographs, informative essays, comprehensive coverage of the sights, and invaluable advice on accommodation, dining and recreation.

Insight Guide: Spain (APA, updated 2004). A comprehensive guide to the country's many facets, with a stunning array of photos, fascinating features and updated travel tips.

The Sun Also Rises (aka *Fiesta*) by Ernest Hemingway (Vintage 1996). The novel that brought Pamplona's fiesta of San Fermín to the world's attention.

The Basque History of the World by Mark Kurlansky (Vintage, 2000). This is a spirited attempt to explain the situation of the Basques today.

Pilgrim Snail by Ben Nimmo (Flamingo, 2001). A personal – and idiosyncratic – account of one man's 2,000-mile, nine-month trek from Canterbury to Santiago, and the diverse characters he meets en route.

The Pilgrimage to Santiago by Edwin Mullins (Signal Books, 2001). An updated edition of one of the classic books about the pilgrimage route.

The Road to Santiago de Compostela by Michael Jacobs (Penguin, 1992). A guide to the architecture on the pilgrimage route.

The New Spaniards by John Hooper (Penguin, updated 1995). An insightful account of all facets of modern Spain, from the complexities of national politics to the arcane rituals of rural villages.

Wildlife Travelling Companion: Spain by John Measures (Crowood Press 1992). A good introduction and guide to Spain's natural attractions.

www.insightguides.com

✳ INSIGHT GUIDES

The World Leader in Visual Travel Guides & Maps

As travellers become ever more discriminating, Insight Guides is using the vast experience gained over three-and-a-half decades of guide-book publishing to create an even wider range of titles to serve them. For those who want the big picture, Insight Guides and Insight City Guides provide comprehensive coverage of a destination. Insight Pocket Guides supply personal recommendations for a short stay. Insight Compact Guides are attractively portable. Insight FlexiMaps are both rugged and easy to use. And specialist titles cover shopping, eating out, and museums and galleries. Wherever you're going, our writers and photographers have already been there – more than once.

ACKNOWLEDGEMENTS

All photography by Bill Wassman except

Lyle Lawson	*10, 13T*
Private Archive	*11, 13B, 15B*
Editions d'Art Devreaux	*14*
Stuart Wallace/Imagestate	*Front cover*
Bill Wassman	*Back Cover*

Tanvir Virdee	*Cover Design*
Maria Donnelly	*Cartography*

© APA Publications GmbH & Co. Verlag KG Singapore Branch, Singapore

Clara Villanueva kindly acted as Spanish language consultant and updater for the project.

Thanks also go to the following individuals and organisations for their help in the research for this book: Hertz, the staff of the Spanish Tourist Office in London, Amparo Garrido, Asun Gómez, Candelas Saenz de Munarriz, Gorka Barguilla, Javier Nebot, Jon Bilbao, Juan Carlos Murillo, Kepa Madariaga, Klaas Schenk, Pily Garrido and Puri Villanueva.

INDEX